THE STATES AND THE NATION SERIES, of which this volume is a part, is designed to assist the American people in a serious look at the ideals they have espoused and the experiences they have undergone in the history of the nation. The content of every volume represents the scholarship, experience, and opinions of its author. The costs of writing and editing were met mainly by grants from the National Endowment for the Humanities, a federal agency. The project was administered by the American Association for State and Local History, a nonprofit learned society, working with an Editorial Board of distinguished editors, authors, and historians, whose names are listed below.

Missouri

A Bicentennial History

Paul C. Nagel

W. W. Norton & Company, Inc.
New York

American Association for State and Local History
Nashville

Copyright © 1977
American Association for State and Local History

All rights reserved

Published and distributed by W. W. Norton & Company, Inc.
500 Fifth Avenue
New York, New York 10036

Printed in the United States of America

Library of Congress Cataloguing-in-Publication Data

Nagel, Paul C
Missouri, a Bicentennial history.

(The States and the Nation series)
Bibliography: p. 193
Includes index.
1. Missouri—History. I. Title. II. Series.
F466.N3   977.8   77–4395
ISBN 0–393–05633–3

2 3 4 5 6 7 8 9 0

*This book is dedicated to the four
generations of my family who from
the 1830s helped to build Missouri. I think especially of my
great great grandparents Blank,
Groenemann, Kloeckner, and Nagel,
my great grandfather, Konrad Johan-
nes Nagel (1826–1903), my grandfather, Gottlieb Johann Nagel (1869–
1953), and my father, Paul Conrad
Nagel (1899–1965).*

Contents

Illustrations

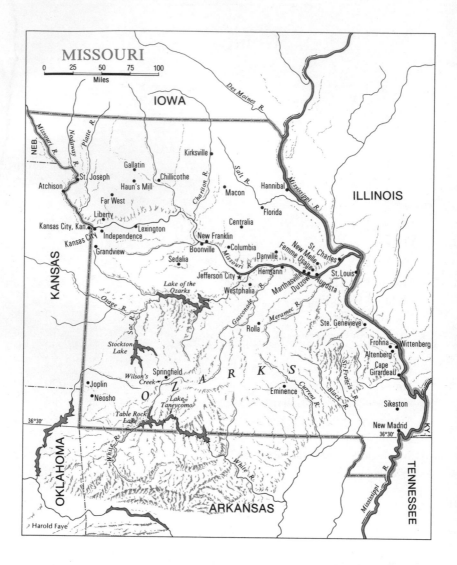

MISSOURI

0   25   50   75   100
    Miles

IOWA

NEB.

Des Moines R.

Nodaway R.
Missouri R.
Platte R.

Kirksville

Gallatin
St. Joseph
Haun's Mill
Atchison
Far West
Liberty

Chillicothe

Salt R.
Chariton R.

Macon

Hannibal

Florida

Mississippi R.

ILLINOIS

Kansas City, Kan.

Kansas City
Grandview
Independence

Lexington

New Franklin
Boonville
Sedalia

Centralia

Columbia

Danville

Femme Osage
New Melle

St. Charles

KANSAS

Lake of the
Ozarks

Jefferson City ★
Westphalia

Missouri R.

Hermann

Marthasville
Dutzow
Augusta

St. Louis

Osage R.

Sac R.

Gasconade R.

Meramec R.

Rolla

Ste. Genevieve

Stockton
Lake

Wilson's
Creek

Springfield

O   Z   A   R   K   S

Joplin
Neosho

Lake
Taneycomo

Table Rock
Lake

36°30'

Eminence

Current R.

Black R.

St. Francis R.

Frohna
Altenberg

Wittenberg

Cape
Girardeau

Sikeston

New Madrid
36°30'

KY.

OKLAHOMA

White R.

White R.

Mississippi R.

TENNESSEE

ARKANSAS

Harold Faye

Invitation to the Reader

IN 1807, former President John Adams argued that a complete history of the American Revolution could not be written until the history of change in each state was known, because the principles of the Revolution were as various as the states that went through it. Two hundred years after the Declaration of Independence, the American nation has spread over a continent and beyond. The states have grown in number from thirteen to fifty. And democratic principles have been interpreted differently in every one of them.

We therefore invite you to consider that the history of your state may have more to do with the bicentennial review of the American Revolution than does the story of Bunker Hill or Valley Forge. The Revolution has continued as Americans extended liberty and democracy over a vast territory. John Adams was right: the states are part of that story, and the story is incomplete without an account of their diversity.

The Declaration of Independence stressed life, liberty, and the pursuit of happiness; accordingly, it shattered the notion of holding new territories in the subordinate status of colonies. The Northwest Ordinance of 1787 set forth a procedure for new states to enter the Union on an equal footing with the old. The Federal Constitution shortly confirmed this novel means of building a nation out of equal states. The step-by-step process through which territories have achieved self-government and national representation is among the most important of the Founding Fathers' legacies.

The method of state-making reconciled the ancient conflict between liberty and empire, resulting in what Thomas Jefferson called an empire for liberty. The system has worked and remains unaltered, despite enormous changes that have taken

ix

place in the nation. The country's extent and variety now sur-
pass anything the patriots of '76 could likely have imagined.
The United States has changed from an agrarian republic into a
highly industrial and urban democracy, from a fledgling nation
into a major world power. As Oliver Wendell Holmes remarked
in 1920, the creators of the nation could not have seen completely how it and its constitution and its states would develop.
Any meaningful review in the bicentennial era must consider
what the country has become, as well as what it was.

The new nation of equal states took as its motto *E Pluribus
Unum*—"out of many, one." But just as many peoples have
become Americans without complete loss of ethnic and cultural
identities, so have the states retained differences of character.
Some have been superficial, expressed in stereotyped images—
big, boastful Texas, "sophisticated" New York, "hillbilly"
Arkansas. Other differences have been more real, sometimes instructively, sometimes amusingly; democracy has embraced
Huey Long's Louisiana, bilingual New Mexico, unicameral Nebraska, and a Texas that once taxed fortunetellers and spawned
politicians called "Woodpecker Republicans" and "Skunk
Democrats." Some differences have been profound, as when
South Carolina secessionists led other states out of the Union in
opposition to abolitionists in Massachusetts and Ohio. The result was a bitter Civil War.

The Revolution's first shots may have sounded in Lexington
and Concord; but fights over what democracy should mean and
who should have independence have erupted from Pennsylvania's Gettysburg to the "Bleeding Kansas" of John Brown,
from the Alamo in Texas to the Indian battles at Montana's
Little Bighorn. Utah Mormons have known the strain of isolation; Hawaiians at Pearl Harbor, the terror of attack; Georgians
during Sherman's march, the sadness of defeat and devastation.
Each state's experience differs instructively; each adds understanding to the whole.

The purpose of this series of books is to make that kind of understanding accessible, in a way that will last in value far
beyond the bicentennial fireworks. The series offers a volume
on every state, plus the District of Columbia—fifty-one, in all.

Each book contains, besides the text, a view of the state through eyes other than the author's—a "photographer's essay," in which a skilled photographer presents his own personal perceptions of the state's contemporary flavor.

We have asked authors not for comprehensive chronicles, nor for research monographs or new data for scholars. Bibliographies and footnotes are minimal. We have asked each author for a summing up—interpretive, sensitive, thoughtful, individual, even personal—of what seems significant about his or her state's history. What distinguishes It? What has mattered about it, to its own people and to the rest of the nation? What has it come to now?

To interpret the states in all their variety, we have sought a variety of backgrounds in authors themselves and have encouraged variety in the approaches they take. They have in common only these things: historical knowledge, writing skill, and strong personal feelings about a particular state. Each has wide latitude for the use of the short space. And if each succeeds, it will be by offering you, in your capacity as a *citizen* of a state *and* of a nation, stimulating insights to test against your own.

James Morton Smith
General Editor

Preface

ANY son of Missouri who writes about his state for the States and the Nation Series faces a precarious if not foolhardy adventure. Volumes in this series seek the character and spirit of each state. Unfortunately, Missouri reveals little about herself that is not varied, confusing, and contradictory. Her story is as often disillusioning as it is inspiring, for her relationship to the Union has been a mixture of triumph, despair, and embarrassment. Even though my forebears have been earnest Missourians since Andrew Jackson's day, my perspective only confirms the elusiveness of Missouri's meaning. I began to watch Missouri as I grew up in Jackson County during the depression era. Then, while living for many years in other parts of the United States, I used a safe distance to think further about Missouri's peculiarities. When I became a Missouri citizen again, my work for a time allowed me to revisit much of the state and her people. None of this consideration, however, has done more for me than confirm Missouri as a bewildering blend of geography, humanity, and events. I am the first to confess that Missouri is difficult to understand.

Nevertheless, the privilege of writing this book requires that I attempt to explain Missouri. The following pages contain my interpretation of what Missouri's history and spirit have implied, both for her people through several generations and for the nation today. Probably any other person who accepted this assign-

ment would write a quite different book. Fortunately, this bicentennial series proceeds on the assumption that to wring the
meaning of any state's story from the tangle of American federalism ought to be a very personal experience and expression.
Mine has surely been that, and I salute the National Endowment
for the Humanities and the American Association for State and
Local History for making the opportunity possible. Those
readers who may be piqued or intrigued by what I have written
should turn to the many other histories of Missouri available, all
of which attempt a more traditional approach. Missouri deserves
larger attention and understanding, and I shall be elated if this
little volume provokes new thought about the state.

I am much indebted to the scholars who have preceded me in
studying Missouri, for without their labor this book could not
have been promptly prepared. Especially am I grateful to the
many citizens, friends, and kinsmen scattered throughout Missouri with whom I talked in hope of deciphering the state.
While all these allies sought to shield me from error, I must
remind every reader that to me alone comes the blame for any
shortcomings in the pages ahead.

Much needed support for the project was given by the University of Missouri, which granted me sabbatical leave during
which this volume was written. I appreciate the encouragement
of Richard S. Brownlee, director of the State Historical Society
of Missouri and his associate, James W. Goodrich. I also heart-
ily thank Gerald George, managing editor of the States and the
Nation Series, and Timothy C. Jacobson, assistant managing
editor for the series, because, having embroiled me in this haz-
ardous enterprise, they did not let me suffer forlorn. I acknowledge a special debt to Phyllis Boechler, Cris Easton, and Ida
Mae Wolff, who typed the manuscript.

This volume was completed because Joan Peterson Nagel
once again helped me overcome the exasperation of writing a
book. Her aid, counsel, and patience were indispensable.
Among her numerous achievements Joan has proven that since a
Minnesota Swede can live with a Missouri German, there may
be a future for the "Show Me" state after all.

P. C. N.

1 August 1976

Missouri

Introduction

$\mathcal{M}$ ISSOURI calls to tourists with the refrain: "Missouri—there's no state quite like it." This is a reasonable appeal. Some journalists make the same point by describing Missouri as America in miniature or microcosm, noting especially her extraordinary variety of settings and citizens. It is just this agglomeration of resources and traditions which promises at the outset that Missouri's history and spirit are unique. Every state doubtless has important differences, but Missouri's experiences have cultivated in her a special quality. To discover this spirit requires moving through the state's tumultuous history as well as through a conflicting array of ancient traditions and folkways, of Ozark Mountains and vast plains, of river hamlets and two warring cities, St. Louis and Kansas City, where most of the state's population now reside. Ultimately it becomes evident that the mood which grips Missouri is one arising from the state's vast countryside and appearing most often in Jefferson City, the small town which the state uses as her capital. Here representatives from the two cities are usually brought under the spell woven by spokesmen from outstate, leaving Kansas City and St. Louis helpless before the larger spirit in Missouri. That spirit—its elements, how it grew out of Missouri's history, and its impact—is the recurring concern of the chapters that follow.

Those who wish to appreciate the physical manifestations of Missouri's spirit must avoid the easy routes across the state. The interstate highways are actually alien creations, and Missouri shows herself only dimly beside them. Missouri is best found by driving along the county routes which move through an infinitely varied scenery. These roads usually lead to county seats—the state has 114, some of which need to be seen before one can appreciate what Missouri means in the 1970s. There, in the center of the town square, sits the once impressive county courthouse. Occasionally the building will have received some modern touches, but these rarely interfere with a brooding mood present in the courthouse square where there have been few changes in a hundred or more years. Around the square are structures often in distress. Broken, dilapidated if still functioning, or boarded up as if to await a summons for new duty, these buildings frequently are vivid reminders of Missouri's story.

These small towns and the countryside around them hint strongly at how, through such ravages as economic depression, civil and guerrilla war, religious dispute, and dwindling population, the ordeal of Missouri's history has implanted in her a disposition which is sure to tug at any person who pauses for a time near a county courthouse. It is a quiet, unpretentious viewpoint, marked by a determination to cherish the old and consider skeptically the new. The essential Missouri quality has been above all this cautious mood, with a people made doubters by what they and their forebears endured in the haste of national development. This spirit, which can best be described as Jeffersonian in character, came increasingly to command the course of Missouri development. No one could have foreseen the singular appropriateness of the choice when Missouri decided to name her new capital city after Thomas Jefferson.

To Missourians, Jeffersonianism has meant a few simple precepts. The state has always harbored doubts about anything associated with a large city. Citizens believed that the good in mankind—such as there was—flourished in a rural setting. As for politics, when men created government, Missourians recognized that it was a risky business. Certainly no state has more sturdily insisted that powers granted to government must be limited. Missouri has seemed especially devoted to the theory that the virtue of government is inversely proportionate to the amount of money which the politicians are permitted to spend.

Generally, Missourians have treasured the Jeffersonian tradition for its negative potential. A mistrust of men and society, an ardent defense of simple, rural life, and a cynical approach to change have often characterized Missouri's mood. These qualities prevailed in Missouri even as America at large seemed intoxicated by talk of assured progress, of human perfectibility, of the advantages of technology, and of the need for vigorous government. In this way Missouri earned her nickname as the "Show Me" state. Events after 1875 convinced many Missourians that "you'll have to show me" was the most positive approach possible in the face of modern conditions. Missouri was left with few illusions.

The old agrarian suspicion of those who hold no property makes it necessary even in the 1970s for large majorities of Missourians to vote their consent before revenue and general obligation bonds can be approved. Many state and local issues still come before the electorate, since most Missourians are convinced that direct government is safer than representative government. County administration remains decentralized, using many officials and often relying on the township system, which among other things means that countywide assessment and collection of taxes is avoided. Many towns prefer to keep fourth-class status, while the prospect of city manager government makes many Missourians highly suspicious. Between local government and the state administration flourishes a kind of conflict and hostility which many citizens consider to be an important means of curtailing the potential evils of both. Meanwhile, if government in much of Missouri is rarely allowed to use professionals, the power of personality, family, and party surely does continue.

Few states have developed so intimate a tie between their history and the mood or character prevailing among their citizens. It is just such a relationship which this book attempts to reconstruct. The nine chapters to follow are essays using several vantage points to follow the development of Missouri's character and spirit within the American Union. The first concern is the place Missouri has filled in American thinking. Novelists, artists, and the popular imagination have used Missouri for many purposes, some of which reveal as much about the nation as about Missouri. This chapter is followed by discussions of Missouri's early years, of her natural advantages, of the different settings which make the state so bewildering, of the variety of people who have claimed to be Missourians, and of the principal events and men most important in Missouri's stewardship for Jeffersonian belief and politics. The state's early career was dominated by the impressive figure of Thomas Hart Benton, and Harry S. Truman overshadowed the later story. Between these periods were years in which Missouri was tormented by several brutal episodes of internal division and violence. The book closes with an examination of how Missouri's imagination has responded to the major forces at work in American life since 1875.

Through more than 150 years of Missouri's statehood run a number of significant themes beyond that of her dedication to a Jeffersonian outlook and to the Democratic party. Her history tells much about the vital but often fickle impact of geography upon a state whose social variety was matched only by her riches in topography and natural resources. Missouri's development was long caught up in the moving frontier, a fact evident in the lore surrounding figures such as Daniel Boone, Lewis and Clark, Kit Carson, and Joseph Smith; and evident also in the prominence of the town called Independence, where for a generation the nation jumped into the awesome great West. Ironically, Missouri's story became one of a people trapped by movement. First acclaimed as "Mother of the West," with sons leaving to found Texas, Oregon, New Mexico, California, and other faraway places, in time the state found that the pattern of national growth was ignoring her.

While St. Louis proudly expected in 1870 to succeed Washington as the nation's capital, railroad, manufacturing, and financial forces soon chose instead to make Chicago America's major inland city. At this point St. Louis and Missouri entered a steady decline in growth and influence, so that within a few decades Missouri had moved from the head of America's national procession to a place far behind. The state was uncomfortable when great cities, national markets, enormous government, and a society consisting of interest blocs overcame a quieter America of small farms, regional economies, simple government, and modest human wants.

Missouri's is a tale of triumph and disappointment, of leadership and retreat, and of color and shabbiness. Experience profoundly touched the state, leaving her appreciative of the values of the early Republic long after many in the nation had forgotten the Founders' hesitations. Consequently, Missouri has been impressed with the mark of history in a significant manner. It is an imprint which the rest of America might study to advantage.

1

Missouri in America's Imagination

*T*HERE is no better way to begin the story of Missouri than to consider how she affected the American imagination. Certainly a state is difficult to resist whose name invokes images as diverse and symbolic as Tom Sawyer and Jesse James, Daniel Boone and Tom Pendergast, the Ozark Hills and the rivermen, as well as the mule and the shimmering steel arch which Eero Saarinen created for the Jefferson National Expansion Memorial on Missouri's eastern shore. Whether by the pen of Samuel Clemens, the brush of George Caleb Bingham, or the flight of Charles Lindbergh's *Spirit of St. Louis,* America has come to Missouri for glimpses of a life and outlook which once seemed so promising when the nation and Missouri were young. It was easy for early Missouri to serve as a setting for several of America's most successful novelists and painters. For a nation increasingly burdened by industrial and urban problems there was some charm in the legendary figures of Jesse James, Tom Pendergast, and the mule, and especially also in the dream world of the great 1904 fair in St. Louis. In these many guises, America has used Missouri to simplify or evade the difficulties which afflicted the nation. Considering that Missouri herself often turned away from America's troubles and withdrew into her own past, her contribution was curiously appropriate.

What America remembers best about Missouri comes from the state's most vigorous days in national affairs, the first half of

9

the nineteenth century. In those early years Missouri seemed to enjoy a happy combination of the splendors of nature and the heroics of men. Timothy Flint was one of the earliest authors to carry Missouri's story across the nation, especially through his raptures over one of the state's great figures, Daniel Boone. Flint made him embody America's cherished courage and resourcefulness in mastering the continent. Boone's relation to Missouri and Kentucky was somewhat more complicated, which became a story of its own. The old pathfinder had come to Missouri filled with disgust at Kentucky where he had been swindled out of his property. Boone insisted his worst fate would be removal from Missouri after death for burial in Kentucky. In later years, however, a contrite Kentucky disputed with Missouri over Boone's bones and finally carried them back to the bluegrass. At least that was the official version. There are Missourians who are confident that Kentucky was carefully given the wrong body, leaving the old pathfinder still asleep in Missouri.

To Boone's legend Missouri added many more tales from the halcyon frontier days. The thrilling expedition of Lewis and Clark from St. Louis to the Pacific Coast was acclaimed as a Missouri feat. The three trails across the plains to Santa Fe, California, and Oregon were an inexhaustible source of inspiring stories. These grand narratives seemed to prove that in Missouri men drew the courage and skills to master the unbelievably difficult paths to the Southwest or to the valleys of the Sacramento and Willamette rivers. Missouri also supplied many tales about the heroes of fur trading and riverboating days, featuring such sons of Missouri as the Sublette brothers, Mike Fink, Jedediah Smith, Kit Carson, Jim Bridger, and "Broken Hand" Fitzpatrick. Especially irresistible was the account of how Fitzpatrick led a group in 1824 which discovered South Pass, the elusive avenue through the Rockies needed for pioneers to travel readily from Missouri across the mountains. Another Missourian, William Ashley, found the Green River in a spectacular and oft-told story. He managed to thrive from the dangers of the fur trader's life and retired to become a congressman from Missouri during the Jacksonian era.

Missouri's prominence in the heyday of fur traders and plains travel gave her a commanding place in much of America's most colorful history. Possibly the most famous episode among these Missouri exploits involved the courage of Alexander Doniphan and his band of Missourians during the Mexican War. Coming from Liberty, a hamlet near Independence, Doniphan led the First Regiment of Missouri Volunteers to Mexico in early summer of 1846. After helping subdue Santa Fe, Doniphan set out with 500 mounted Missourians from the Rio Grande River to cross ninety miles of desert known to the natives as "Dead Man's Journey." Near El Paso, this wretchedly clad and poorly supplied detachment confronted a larger, well-equipped Mexican army which announced its intent of putting every Missourian to the sword. The battle of El Brazito saw Doniphan's ragamuffins easily defeat the Mexicans. To the satisfaction of American readers, this feat meant the slaughter of many Mexican soldiers with not a Missourian lost.

After capturing El Paso, the Missourians briefly enjoyed the food and ladies of that town before turning toward Chihuahua, 300 miles to the south. During February 1847, Doniphan's men moved through blowing sand, the smoke of prairie fires, and intense heat to the Sacramento River, where they met a Mexican force nearly five times their size. Using tactics familiar to Missouri traders accustomed to being outnumbered during Indian assaults, the Missouri regiment killed or wounded 800 Mexicans while suffering few casualties. After capturing Chihuahua in early March, the astonishing Missourians then faced the most difficult part of their ordeal, an exhausting struggle across 600 miles. Finally, Doniphan and his men reached the main American army at Buena Vista, where they decided not to re-enlist but to go home. When the First Missouri Regiment entered New Orleans, clad literally in shreds, it was already a national legend.

The June 1847 trip from New Orleans to St. Louis was a triumphal tour, with citizens all along the river celebrating the unbelievable accomplishments of Doniphan's band. The Missourians had marched over two thousand agonizing miles and defeated foes far more numerous than they, losing only four men to death in battle. In satisfying America's hungry imagination, the achievement of Doniphan and his men was unmatched. It became the last great chapter in Missouri's frontier lore, although it had a modest rival in the courage of the Pony Express riders a few years later. Not until Charles A. Lindbergh flew the *Spirit of St. Louis* alone from New York to Paris did Missouri heroism again hold the national attention. Lindbergh's feat in 1927 had a century-old quality which reminded America of the times when Missouri and other western states had shown vividly how individual courage and energy could overcome insurmountable barriers.

While Missouri's legends certainly did their share for the national faith according to the canons of American wholesomeness, they also catered to a more perverse sense of what the nation's unbridled spirit was supposed to mean. Of the many striking figures to linger from Missouri's past, few had a broader appeal than the thief and murderer, Jesse James. Between 1875 and 1882, once-proud Missouri shrank under the national epithet of the "robber state." Those dismal years climaxed a generation of internal violence which began with the border warfare over slavery in the 1850s. Missouri's tragic vexation by gangs like the one of the James brothers eventually became the setting out of which the nation assuaged its hunger for tales of daring men who could do wrong in order to achieve good ends.

The James brothers, Jesse and Frank, made the pillaged area of western Missouri their land. They knew it well, for they had participated in the wartime guerrilla lawlessness. Competing with at least three other gangs, the James band rode openly until 1880, producing such national editorial refrains as "poor old Missouri." Jesse's gang succeeded in at least fourteen bank robberies, the holdup of the Kansas City Fair, and in train robberies too numerous to count. Murder was a familiar feature of these crimes.

The transformation of such a grisly story into a national legend began in 1881. As the plague of killing, ambush, and robbery grew, Democratic Gov. Thomas T. Crittenden, once an officer in the Union cavalry, adopted controversial tactics to stop the James outfit. Missouri statutes limited Governor Crittenden to paying only $300 of public money as reward for captured criminals. However, the besieged railroads offered the governor $50,000 for use in apprehending the pesky James boys. Immediately, Crittenden proclaimed a $5,000 reward for arresting Jesse, with a similar amount to be paid upon the bandit's conviction for robbery or murder. The same price was offered for Frank James.

During the winter of 1881–1882, little occurred except more daring activity by the James boys and criticism of Crittenden for taking money from the widely unpopular railroads. Then, in April 1882, Crittenden's scheme began to succeed, but in ways the governor could hardly have anticipated. As America watched in disbelief, the James brothers' career ended and their saga began when two members of Jesse's gang, Robert and Charles Ford, found the reward money irresistible. With county officials, they allegedly contrived a plot which began with Bob Ford pretending to visit Jesse in his St. Joseph hideout and shooting him in the back of the head. The assassins immediately surrendered to local authorities and were tried, convicted, and sentenced to hang for the killing. The Fords were then pardoned by Governor Crittenden, bringing about an uproar because of the suspicion that the governor had contracted with criminals to slay Jesse James. Astonishment was heightened when Frank James closed his days of crime by presenting himself quietly to the governor in the capitol. Indignation grew when Crittenden acknowledged he had paid $20,000 to end the career of the James boys, but the governor refused to reveal the recipients of the reward.

While the governor argued that the affair was a bargain with the money not even coming from the public's pocket, the widening outcry over Crittenden's method established a new heroism around the dead bandit and his accomplices. The memory of the bloodshed and pillaging of the outlaws was forgotten and instead the manner of Jesse's betrayal was remembered. A popular ballad closed with the suggestion that Jesse met a purifying fate under his alias, "Thomas Howard."

> Jesse James was a lad that killed many a man.
> He robbed the Danville train,

But the dirty little coward that killed Mr. Howard,
Has laid poor Jesse in his grave.

Soon after retirement of the James family to legendary
realms, another Missouri clan began a career which also drew
national attention. Not only did the Pendergast family master
Kansas City, but (according to rumor) they ruled most of Missouri by the 1930s. Building upon an older brother's organization, Thomas J. Pendergast dominated Kansas City from 1924
until the federal penitentiary claimed him in 1939. During those
years the nation was tempted to imagine Missouri as an axis
turning between the extremes of natural goodness in the sublime
Ozark Hills and collapsed political and social dignity in Kansas
City. Within this paradox Tom Pendergast's career made fascinating journalism for American readers.

The Pendergast power stemmed from skillful ability in pull-
ing economic strings, exploiting relationships between police
and vice racketeers, exhuming names of long-deceased voters at
election time, and paying attention to the needs of residents in
important precincts. None of this was novel except perhaps for
the diverting manner in which the Pendergast system functioned. Thus, for many Americans who visited Kansas City, one
of the great national wonders was the amount of concrete used
in the town. Even the bed of Brush Creek, which meandered
through the Country Club district, was paved. Tom Pendergast's
premix concrete company admittedly put out good material, but
its wide use was phenomenal. Equally famed beyond Kansas
City was Pendergast's simple second floor office above a store
on Main Street. Here, each morning, sitting at an old desk and
inevitably wearing his hat, the boss met anyone who cared to
call, thoughtfully listening to the needs or complaints of unknown citizens or to the concerns of those in high places in the
city and the state.

Accounts of Pendergast's role in Missouri led to a debate of
the mix of evils and advantages inherent in organization politics. Apologists for the machine noted the comfort it gave to
lonely members of a big city community, as well as the progress
and efficiency it appeared to achieve in administration. These

qualities seemed especially appealing during the depression years after 1929 when Pendergast was most successful. Self-styled realists in Missouri and America insisted that the Kansas City situation showed how modern democracy must blend the good and evil found in man and his society. Consequently, in the 1930s, many Kansas City citizens preferred to gaze up at the handsome new buildings Pendergast had caused to rise among them, and thus to look away from the gangland-style murders occurring on the streets around them.

In the end it was not his interpretation of democracy which dislodged Tom Pendergast. While he had grown wealthy from the remarkable coincidence between his family's concrete, asphalt, pipe, oil, and garbage business interests and the public's needs, nothing had been strictly illicit in his commercial practices. However, Pendergast's income was insufficient to pay for his compulsion to gamble. Eventually he accepted money which he failed to report to the Bureau of Internal Revenue, an omission for which he went to prison in 1939.

Tom Pendergast and the many other figures in these legends about Missourians in exploration, trade, trapping, war, robbery, and bossism had to make room, however, for the even broader appeal growing from portraits of uncomplicated times and boyhood scenes. The Missouri which most Americans have carried in their minds was created by Samuel L. Clemens, the state's most famous author. Writing as Mark Twain, Sam Clemens answered his own emotional needs and those of generations of readers by retreating into a world of youthful simplicity and unspoiled nature. This Missouri of *Tom Sawyer* and *Huckleberry Finn* was recreated just as America, around 1880, entered an age of industrial and finance capitalism. Tom and Huck took readers back to scenes where the best in the nation's tradition was presumed to thrive.

Critics have debated what subtle symbols or meanings Clemens may have woven into the pages of his novels about Missouri boyhood. However, all agree that fundamentally the books offer a moving, nostalgic glimpse of a cherished world which Americans were forgetting in their rush toward progress. Consequently, both Missouri and Sam Clemens came to serve the paradox in America's culture, which required material conquest while leaving the natural charm of America unvexed. Clemens himself was keenly aware of what was happening to the land and to the citizens' soul. Yet, amid mounting political and economic degradation after 1875, most Americans wanted some inducement to believe that human nature was still as simple, straightforward, and perfectible as that of young lads living in the charm of Missouri's rural and village beauty. It was a world Americans insisted they would never totally abandon or seriously desecrate.

Although he spent his adult years in New England, Clemens apparently found the memory of his Missouri boyhood irresistible. He grew up in the area now known as Little Dixie, which to some observers has been closest to the essential spirit of the state. Young Sam knew from the beginning about rivers, about blacks as servants, and especially about the languid, cautious outlook of the villages and small farms whose inhabitants had much of Kentucky and Virginia in their family records. The older he became, the more ardent was Clemens's nostalgia for his world of Monroe and Marion counties. He was fond of saying that every force which created his being was in a Missouri village. To the widow of a boyhood chum, he wrote that he yearned to relive his youth and then drown.

While the mildest inducement made Clemens turn his thoughts to days in Hannibal, Missouri, he recognized the dangers and human shortcomings which even the Missouri hamlets of Florida and Hannibal harbored in the 1840s. He remembered the descent into genteel poverty which the exodus to Missouri brought so many hopeful migrants from Kentucky and elsewhere. He could recall his family's veneration for a dreary Tennessee land investment which his hapless father, John Marshall Clemens, insisted would eventually lift the family to Missouri eminence. Young Sam knew how his father had shared the futile dreams of other men settled along the Salt River, believing improvements in its navigability would transform that rustic region of Missouri into exciting prosperity. However, even a half-century after Sam Clemens died, Florida, Missouri, remained largely unchanged from the primal state in which her famous son was a lad.

Tom Sawyer, published in 1876, and *Huckleberry Finn,* published in 1884, assured that Hannibal, Missouri, would for generations of Americans, young and old, be an imaginary refuge from the disappointments of modern America. Samuel Clemens was soon joined by three other novelists who enlarged the links between Missouri and America's imagination. The three— E. W. Howe, Harold Bell Wright, and Winston Churchill— each used Missouri very differently as a setting and a tradition in appealing to the expanding numbers of American readers. Each had a personal association with the state which marked his work. The three authors were so successful in their popular sales that Missouri long continued one of the most familiar states to American readers, many of whom had first heard of the area through the voices of Huck Finn and Tom Sawyer.

Although Howe, Wright, and Churchill were less masterful artists than Clemens, their approaches to Missouri represented the three appeals most evident in American literature. Churchill adroitly played upon America's yearning for the past. Wright pitted the goodness of nature and Christian virtue against urban grasping and intellectual pride. Howe pioneered by candidly describing the purportedly idyllic life of the farm and the village. In all three approaches—historical romance, simplistic moralism, and honest realism—Missouri served as the inspiration for a trio of the nation's most widely read authors.

Of the three, the earliest efforts were by Ed Howe, who wrote *The Story of a Country Town,* a blunt recounting of the life he knew as a youth in Bethany, a hamlet in northwest Missouri across the state from Clemens's village of Hannibal. The book appeared in 1883, at first privately published before Howe was thirty years old. He had by then fled a few miles west to the Kansas border town of Atchison, where he became a successful newspaper editor. By 1900, his portrayal of small-town Missouri set in the 1860s and 1870s had gone through forty printings. Howe had sent the novel to Samuel Clemens, telling him that since it was a Missouri story, he might like to read it. He also presented a copy to William Dean Howells, a close friend of Clemens and the nation's leading commentator on literary affairs.

Both Clemens and Howells applauded Howe's picture of Missouri, even though its colors and lines differed sharply in effect from those of Clemens's work. Howe shared Clemens's grim view of man's nature, a view that spilled across the pages of *The Story of a Country Town*. Yet Howe told Clemens that he despised the book. Obviously embarrassed by its technical and literary difficulties, Howe explained that, like so many Missouri boys, his education had been neglected. Nevertheless, William Dean Howells insisted that Howe's accuracy in describing a Missouri rural village contributed something new and vital to American writing. His study of a Missouri village became the bitter beginning to America's literary rebellion against the small town.

In Twin Mounds, as Howe called his community, there was nothing of the West as a second Eden. Instead, it was a locale obsessed with small financial gain and large hatreds built upon a narrowing religious restraint. The endless demands of agricultural existence made a grim backdrop before which was placed the crudeness, spitefulness, thriftlessness, and idleness of small-town existence. The novel suggested that for village Missourians, life was full when it contained quarrels over the Bible, trivial business success, and occasional terms on the town's council. It was also evident that any real success meant escape for the lucky to the East. In Howe's opinion, the poor, indigent, and sick came to Missouri and the West, staying there only if they could do no better.

Perhaps the feature which attracted serious readers to *The Story of a Country Town* was its glimpse of Missouri's character, and thereby that of most other rural societies. In Twin Mounds, and on its adjacent farms, life was exposed and naked. Absent was the advantage of the city where numbers of people and social artifices tempted persons to believe they could hide from one another. Consequently, the meanness and cruelty depicted by Howe were ready companions to the caution gripping the countryside. The occasional embrace of some panacea such as silver coinage, the railroad, or the Grange, seemed usually to spring from recognition of man's limitations. Although Ed Howe's earnest view of Missouri was harsh, its success was enduring among thoughtful students of American life so that in 1961, the novel was republished in a scholarly edition by the Harvard University Press.

Far more enduring popular acclaim came to the stories of Missouri by Harold Bell Wright. Two of his novels did more, perhaps, to fix Missouri in the imagination of America than any other artistic force except that of Sam Clemens. Wright drew on his dislike of intellectualism, materialism, and urbanism to make the glorious topography and human simplicity found in Missouri's hill country a basis for diatribes against early twentieth-century America. As a young adult, Wright came to Missouri from Ohio in 1895. Eventually, his perpetual fight against bronchial disease took him to the Southwest. Although he lived for a time in Missouri's small towns and in Kansas City, Wright's happiest days were spent preaching and writing amid the people of the Ozark hill country. His most famous book, *The Shepherd of the Hills,* completed in 1907, was written while Wright camped on hilltops in southern Missouri. By collaborating with an early master of literary advertising, Wright helped his books to sales of more than ten million copies. While Wright's stories had little to commend them strictly as literature except for a talented rendering of local dialect and lore, they were marvelously suited to comfort souls troubled by a progressive age. Wright dissented from the viewpoint of Theodore Roosevelt and others that America could somehow go forward toward greater wealth and power without the stains brought to national life in the name of industrial and urban progress.

Harold Bell Wright argued that modern circumstance was a snare and delusion. For the countless citizens who felt ensnared and deluded, *The Shepherd of the Hills* and *The Calling of Dan Matthews* offered a reassuring if remote alternative. Wright's story was the transformation in body and spirit of a sophisticated but jaded clergyman from a great city who sought asylum in Missouri's hills and found a paradise. The novels are barely disguised sermons, endlessly explaining how life in the unspoiled out-of-doors, guided by an energetic Christianity and hard work, was as ennobling and satisfying as urban existence was corrupting and dismaying. These themes were hardly new. However, for many thwarted souls Wright's skillful use of highly appealing Missouri props evidently gave freshness to a familiar doctrine. The moral superiority of country folk with their instinctive grasp of Christian precepts may have been the purest form of anti-intellectualism, but Wright's version of Missouri scenes and life appeared to many readers as the truth about America.

Despite its attempt to reduce human concerns to the simplest terms, Wright's story of the city sophisticate who became an Ozark shepherd did not avoid an ambiguous and uneasy conclusion: the hills echo with sounds of blasting and of falling rock as newcomers tear through the mountains to build a railroad. Wright used this familiar literary device to warn that even the nobility of Missouri's hills and people could be destroyed. Should such desecration happen to Missouri, where God had been most loving, the author suggested America would have no place to go to renew itself. Instead, the old shepherd, near death, predicts that the machine will bring people to corrode this Missouri Eden by revelry and idleness. The once great urban intellectual dies, asserting his happiness at escaping the Missouri to come.

Wright's stories held the attention mostly of rural and small-town readers. After 1918, his appeal diminished markedly. Nevertheless, the public continued to follow these tales of Ozark life so that *The Shepherd of the Hills* had a career in paperback edition after World War II. By 1976, Wright's grim prophecy had been realized, but with an ironic touch. His renowned tales of Ozark life were employed to bring strangers flocking to the region. Television ads, accompanied by garish country music, urged everyone to come to the Shepherd of the Hills Country. Upon arriving, the tourist had no trouble spending money, including taking a jeep train on an invasion into the hillsides. At night, a company of seventy actors recreated scenes from the novel. The old shepherd had foreseen more clearly than even Wright could have guessed that no rest was possible for the hills.

More optimistic beliefs about humanity in Missouri and the United States were held by Winston Churchill. After growing up in St. Louis, he went to the New Hampshire hills where his writing brought him wealth. Before he put aside his pen in 1917, Churchill put St. Louis's first century into best sellers. Unlike Howe and Wright, Churchill used the excitement of Missouri history to convey his faith in progress and the eventual greatness of America. His most successful novel, *The Crisis*, published in 1901, told of Civil War life in the St. Louis area with a knowledge of the city and its variety of people that made the book one of America's most enduring historical novels. The author's greatest strength lay in balancing the outlooks and manners of the Germans, Southerners, and New Englanders who struggled in St. Louis during the Civil War. Churchill clearly wanted to use Missouri to show how great and varied streams of human immigration could meet and combine.

Three years later, Churchill completed *The Crossing*, another success which this time stressed eighteenth-century St. Louis, as well as points south on the Mississippi. Ending his novel on the day the United States claimed the city and upper Louisiana, Churchill again displayed a warm affection for the people of Missouri, paying special tribute to the French and their descendants who had founded the Missouri country. While Churchill enjoyed reminding his readers that God had reserved for the United States a high earthly destiny, even he left slightly ajar the possibility that men might falter before such a prospect. Although this may have been a conventional pose, nevertheless Churchill closed *The Crossing* with the hero looking west across Missouri, musing upon what the vast new region might mean for the Republic. Had it indeed been divinely preserved for the American people? Would the nation's precepts prevail, Churchill asked, or would the lust for power and gain debase the future promised by the land beyond St. Louis? Since Churchill wrote when political corruption in St. Louis had become a national scandal, he safely concluded by acknowledging that no

one could say certainly that even in Missouri men would measure up to the Republic.

Because of Clemens, Howe, Wright, and Churchill, Missouri
served for half a century as a setting for literary presentations
read by millions of citizens. After these four authors finished,
no one succeeded in continuing the literary homage to Missouri.
This lapse did not apply, however, to the visual arts, where Missouri had more enduring attention. In each of Missouri's two
centuries of existence a distinguished painter chose to remain a
citizen of the state while bringing to the American imagination
portraits of Missouri scenes and people. George Caleb Bingham
and Thomas Hart Benton, great-nephew of Sen. Thomas H.
Benton, were two of the nation's most successful artists who,
under very different circumstances, advocated American settings as the subject of artistry. While their paintings, especially
those of Benton, were sometimes said to be deficient aestheti-
cally, Bingham and Benton persisted in portraying life as it was,
a conservative approach peculiarly appropriate for two painters
from Missouri.

George Caleb Bingham was part of the Virginia exodus
which reached Missouri before statehood was granted in 1821.
After growing up along the Missouri River, Bingham began
using large canvas to depict life in his area. His *Jolly Flatboat-
men* became one of the enduring glimpses of a cherished episode in American history. Meantime, Bingham remained an active citizen, serving in the Missouri General Assembly, as state
treasurer, and as president of the Kansas City Board of Police
Commissioners. Appropriately, therefore, the most renowned
results of his artistry described the political scene in Missouri.
Especially eloquent were his *Stump Speaking* and *Verdict of the
People*. Bingham's *Order No. 11,* showing the harsh social
realities of the Civil War in western Missouri, was one of the
great expressions of outraged indignation to be put before the
nation.

Bingham thrived as a portrait painter and sketch master, so
much so that he was known in some circles as "The American
Artist." His supporters acclaimed him as a painter who had
transcended the old masters, despite the obvious influence of

seventeenth-century European art which Bingham had studied in St. Louis and in Europe. Whether Bingham succeeded in forming the American school claimed by his friends is debatable, but he undoubtedly offered the American people much of the earnestness and humor of life in youthful Missouri. His scenes thus became a moving reminder of how unpretentious the democratic process was in his state.

Exactly a century after Bingham's career, Thomas Hart Benton brought another Missouri to American audiences. As a son of a congressman, Benton lived in both Neosho, Missouri, and Washington, D.C., where association in the latter city with figures such as William Jennings Bryan and Champ Clark merely fired his determination to disobey his father's order to pursue the law and politics. After studying at the Chicago Art Institute and in Paris, Benton began a career with the belief that candor about life was most important and that beauty rested in things as they were. It was an outlook which Bingham would have applauded. Unlike many sensitive sons of Missouri, Benton returned in 1935 to settle in his state, where he immediately created a furor by murals he was commissioned to paint in the capitol. Nevertheless, the walls of the house lounge became alive with Missouri history as Huck Finn and Tom Sawyer appeared along with the bandit James brothers and Tom Pendergast. Most distressing to some viewers, however, was Benton's stark view of life in Missouri, extending from the two great cities to the villages and to the farms. The completeness and candor were more than even Missourians bargained for, so that controversy followed Benton until his death in 1975 at the age of 85.

One of Benton's most notable paintings, which had to find refuge in New York City, was *Persephone,* showing a naked Missouri girl about to be hauled off to Hades on an old farm wagon hitched to two Missouri mules. The King of the Underworld was none other than a bedraggled Missouri farmer. When the painting first appeared in a New York night spot, nearly forty thousand persons within three weeks came to share this glimpse of Missouri's spirit. Later, however, Americans by the millions arrived in Independence to see Benton's masterpiece depicting Missouri's central role in the opening of the West. This mural was painted between 1959 and 1962 for the Truman Library.

Benton's murals, as with such of his paintings as *Roasting Ears, Cotton Pickers, Lonesome Road,* and *Homestead,* were obviously intended to capture both the natural and the human situation, so that many critics considered Benton less an artist than a grotesque pictorialist. For Missouri, which became accustomed to his bluntness, Benton remained all his long life a gifted son who never forgot the figures and scenes from the state's spectacular early days as well as difficult recent times. Out of both sources, Benton was able to show America how he saw the soul of his state.

The passing of the old Missouri which Clemens, Bingham, and Benton loved was best marked by the fate of the mule. The hybrid offspring of a donkey and a mare, this remarkable animal's growth in fame and value embraced the quality of Missouri and her kingdom of small farmers. By 1870 Missouri produced more mules than any other state, and by 1900 the animal bred in Missouri was not only considered the best in the world, but was universally associated with the state. Missouri could have done far worse than claim the mule as symbol, there being hardly a more amazing creature. Missouri mules were renowned for their great power of endurance, their strength, their simple diet, their refusal to overeat, their excellent health, and their sure feet, which rarely required the blacksmith's attention. Most persons valued mules for their stoic disposition, although the mules themselves shrewdly decided when and how it was best to work. Mules might be stubborn at times, but they were never stupid, so that they were hailed for working endlessly with a phlegmatic patience.

Mules were Missouri's finest contribution to agriculture before machinery pushed them aside. The animals were especially cherished all along the battlefront during World War I in an era when they had their finest moment. There were 440,000 mules on Missouri farms alone in 1922, with countless others found throughout America and the world. Even so, mules, like the stolid small farmers of Missouri, soon began to retreat before the presumed economies and efficiencies of machines and massive cultivation. By 1960 there were fewer than 20,000 mules in the state, most of those being show animals, while much of the breeding stock was sold to toil on new frontiers in South America. For the general imagination, however, the mule lingered as an emblem of traits and times which neither Missouri nor much of America wished to forget.

Another feature of Missouri was nearly as independent and proud as the mule—St. Louis, a city which often seemed to behave as if it had more right to American attention than did Missouri herself. The history of St. Louis preceded Missouri's and was no less colorful or difficult. A dynamic city that wished little association with the state, St. Louis contributed material and intellectual leadership to America until the 1890s. In the 1870s, however, while the city expected momentarily to become the new federal capital, decay set in and within three decades some observers said St. Louis led only in political corruption. Despite these thwarted hopes and profound embarrassments, St. Louis did have a remarkable impact on America's imagination, an impact due in no small degree to the Eliot family, of whom Thomas Stearns Eliot, poet, dramatist, and critic, made a contribution to Anglo-American literature unexcelled in his day.

Although T. S. Eliot emigrated to England at the time of World War I, he occasionally returned to the city and state where his family's career had been highly significant. His grandfather, William Greenleaf Eliot, arrived in St. Louis in 1834 to become one of the most successful intellectual forces in the city and perhaps the state. At first William Eliot's sensitive New England spirit was uneasy amidst the cultural variety in St. Louis during Andrew Jackson's time, for he served as a Unitarian clergyman in this nominally Roman Catholic town which seemed devoutly dedicated mostly to gambling, drunkenness, duelling, and, especially, the pursuit of wealth. Eliot decided to devote his life to forestalling what he considered the gravest threat to Missouri and the new West—that education and letters, religion and morality, all would be crushed by the lust for money.

Consequently, William Eliot gave his remarkable best to the cause of the mind and the spirit in St. Louis, while also assisting in various social causes. Eventually, he became the first president of Washington University, which from the outset numerous Missourians acclaimed as a fit companion for the more renowned colleges on the Atlantic coast. Henry Ware Eliot, father of T. S. Eliot and son of William, carried forward the family's tradition of service, especially by remaining on Washington University's board from 1877 to 1919. Within such a family circle T. S. Eliot was born in 1888. By his own confession, Eliot was never able to forget the Missouri of rivers and cardinal birds, and the old city of St. Louis, saying that Missouri and the Mississippi River made a deeper impression on him than any other part of the world. His most celebrated figure, J. Alfred Prufrock, had a furniture store in St. Louis. That city, Eliot recalled, was for himself a better place to have been born than Boston, New York, or London.

However, the fertility of St. Louis exceeded merely the rearing of such varied literary figures as T. S. Eliot, Winston Churchill, and Eugene Field, the last the author of those highly popular lines, "Little Boy Blue" and "Wynken, Blynken, and Nod." It was also residence for two important journals, the *Journal of Speculative Philosophy* and *Reedy's Mirror,* neither of which deeply affected Missouri's history but which were influential in the nation's intellectual circles. The *Journal of Speculative Philosophy,* published from 1867 to 1893, reflected the zeal of St. Louis Germans for philosophy. Especially important were the efforts of Henry C. Brokmeyer and others who shared his enthusiasm for authors unknown to most Missourians, such as Johann Gottlieb Fichte and of course the impenetrable Georg Wilhelm Friedrich Hegel. This group founded the St. Louis Philosophical Society, which welcomed a New Englander, William T. Harris, as the brilliant editor for the Society's *Journal* and as eventual leader for education in Missouri and the nation. From this spirit in the late nineteenth century, St. Louis emerged briefly as the most exciting place in America for philosophical speculation.

The *Journal* became a forum for figures such as William

James, Josiah Royce, and John Dewey. A procession of distinguished thinkers and writers crossed into Missouri to exchange ideas with Brokmeyer and Harris, as well as with Adolph E. Kroeger, J. Gabriel Woerner, Denton J. Snider, and Dr. Alexander De Menil. Snider alone published fifty volumes on an astonishing range of topics, including eventually the sobering story of St. Louis's rise and decline as the nation's center for philosophy. For a generation persons with specialized appetites could find in St. Louis meetings of many intellectual circles so that the Philosophical Society had to compete with a Hegel Club and a Kant Club for the attention of citizens and guests. St. Louis began retreating as a national cultural leader in the 1890s, partly because William T. Harris returned to his cherished New England, but more from the sudden slump in growth experienced by the city, a growth that devastated the Hegelians who had preached that the movement of irresistible process was bearing St. Louis to a position of supremacy in America.

Still, philosophy's decline did not mark St. Louis's withdrawal entirely from the national literary scene since the career of *Reedy's Mirror* allowed the city some continued claim upon the American imagination. Until the death in 1920 of its editor, William Marion Reedy, the *Mirror* managed to combine critical commentary on the dreadful state of St. Louis's public affairs with an appreciative review of many of the city's finest new writers and poets. During his quarter-century of writing, editing, and publishing, Reedy's singular effort saved St. Louis from suffering the stigma of decadence. Reedy's person and personal life were colorful in the extreme, leading many in St. Louis society to find him disconcerting, especially in view of his long romance and marriage with the woman who operated the finest brothel available during the 1904 exposition. Nevertheless, Reedy was a national voice who had a wide audience, for his charges that St. Louis and the nation were being destroyed by avarice were carried in the *Mirror,* which had a circulation nearly five times that of the *Atlantic* and almost three times that of the *Nation.* Accustomed to luncheon invitations to the White House and to frequent talks with Theodore Roosevelt, Reedy was an international authority on poetry, serving on the committee which selected the first poet to win a Pulitzer Prize.

After devoting its early energies more to political concerns, the *Mirror's* last years concentrated on broadening America's literary perspective. Reedy introduced to the United States such St. Louis writers as Fannie Hurst, Zoë Akins, and Sara Teasdale, who won the first Pulitzer Prize as a poet despite the fact that prize committee member Reedy preferred another choice. Because of Reedy's insistence, Edgar Lee Masters published his *Spoon River Anthology,* while at the same time the *Mirror* was bringing to the fore forgotten authors like Nathaniel Hawthorne; and also new authors, such as Emily Dickinson, Theodore Dreiser, and William Butler Yeats. The *Mirror* presented English authors as well—John Galsworthy, Joseph Conrad, and the Sitwells. In its attempt to cultivate literary taste, Reedy steadfastly emphasized the tie between letters and life, scoffing at William Harris and his band of St. Louis Hegelians, whom Reedy considered pitifully remote and obscure. The message Reedy sent forth from Missouri was that the imaginative life need never be estranged from the tavern, the attorney's office, or the countinghouse.

Such an outlook encouraged an event in 1904 which proved to be Missouri's most successful attempt to command the nation's attention. The proposal for the Louisiana Purchase Universal Exposition had been instigated by civic anger when Chicago earlier won the right to hold the great Columbian Exposition which St. Louis had coveted. To many irate Missourians, remedying this grievance was enough to make them forget that St. Louis's water was often undrinkable, or the air usually impure, or that public utilities were prisoners of private profit. Out of this frustration, Missouri and St. Louis, led by former Gov. David R. Francis, produced the wide co-operation needed to commemorate properly the centennial of the Louisiana Purchase. First, all the states within the purchase area were persuaded to consent in solemn convention that Missouri should be host to the world through the exposition at St. Louis. Then the Missouri constitution was swiftly amended to permit the use of public money for the great occasion, while Congress granted $5 million to the fair with the proviso that it not desecrate the Sabbath. With Missouri's prompting, sixty-two nations and every state except Delaware prepared exhibitions for the fifteen "palaces" on such subjects as mining, art, electricity, and physical culture. Eventually, each state and nation had its own structure, all surrounding Missouri's building, under whose golden dome the state tried to renew a battered belief that she possessed the strength to thrive in all arts and sciences.

When the great exposition finally opened in 1904 after a year's delay, St. Louis had the world's attention. Everyone sang the lyrics of "Meet Me in St. Louiee." It was said with justification that St. Louis enchanted the world, for the fair was a huge success with receipts of $32 million against a cost of $18 million. Twenty million persons came to the fairgrounds, where they sampled the newly invented ice cream cone and ice tea. Visitors were advised to plan a stay of two weeks in order to see everything since in the agricultural building alone a spectator could walk past nine miles of different sights.

Three-quarters of a century later, a more enduring presence had been placed in St. Louis to reflect America's persisting need for reassurance about movement and growth. It was the great arch astride the Jefferson National Expansion Memorial. Designed by the famed Eero Saarinen, this shimmering, beautiful, 17,000-ton curve of steel soared to 630 feet on eighty acres of the land where St. Louis first stood. For the 1970s, the "Gateway Arch" became America's finest representation of the lore about courageous men enjoying the bounty of unspoiled nature. It also spoke of how the nation's momentum and hope had once concentrated upon Missouri and her mighty rivers, a consoling reminder especially for those who fled from the Watergate era into a past where Missouri had once seemed to promise the United States dominion over a limitless new future.

Given Missouri's central role in that idealized America of great rivers, vast countryside, and steadfast pioneers, the arch at St. Louis handsomely embodies the state's principal place in the American imagination. It also marks the spot where the nation's two noblest rivers join. Here began not only Missouri's history but also her brief time of national leadership.

2

Child of Three Empires

$\mathcal{U}$ PON entering the Union in 1821, Missouri closed an astonishing career in the western empires of France, Spain, and the United States. Such an exciting youth convinced many Americans—and surely most early Missourians—that the new state was marked for a special role in American affairs. No one had more expectations for the Missouri region than did President Thomas Jefferson, who purchased it from France in 1803. Long before becoming president in 1801 Jefferson had been keenly interested in western America, and especially in the mysterious realm beyond the Mississippi. However, the president was as startled as anyone when his purchase brought the United States ownership of a region stretching a thousand miles from New Orleans up the Mississippi to St. Louis and beyond. Swiftly responding to this amazing windfall Jefferson began to arrange the Missouri region's future and immediately made one of his rare blunders by overlooking the fact that Missouri had a past as well as a future. He did not realize that the Missouri country held more than ten thousand persons of whom probably 1,500 were black. Established in 1764, St. Louis contained gentlemen, hunters, merchants, boatmen, former soldiers, and Indians, to say nothing of the charming Creole women. Outside the town were the farms which refugees from the United States had preferred.

The president received the breathtaking news of the Louisiana

Purchase in the summer of 1803 while he was at Monticello, his beloved home in Virginia. There, amid the well-established pattern of Virginia society and far from the bustle around St. Louis, Jefferson decided to impose order upon the new West. The president knew that south of the mouth of the Arkansas River, the region which included New Orleans was already partially settled and therefore its climate, geography, and resources known. To the north, however, Jefferson expected a free hand in shaping the next century of American growth. He was especially eager to remove the Indian tribes from locations where they conflicted with white settlement. Believing that America's original domain east of the Mississippi River afforded ample growing space for the nation's white civilization, Jefferson took the acquisition of the Missouri country as the solution to the future of the red man.

To his advisers the president proposed a dramatic plan. White settlers who had entered Missouri under the French and Spanish would withdraw eastward across the Mississippi and all Indian tribes would then be taken westward into Missouri. There, safely remote from white men, Jefferson expected the Indians to change their culture from hunting and fighting to farming and herding. During the time it took for them to become "civilized," Jefferson saw the Indian presence as a buffer between the United States and the Spanish and English empires which lay beyond.

One of the delightful ironies about Missouri's early history, therefore, is that the president whom Missourians came to revere as their great patron and for whom they would name their capital city intended to order white settlement to retreat from Missouri. Jefferson's first wish was to delay, perhaps for a century, the establishment of American life in Missouri. Peering westward into little-known Missouri from his quiet retreat at Monticello, Jefferson dreamed of a slow, deliberate movement of America's frontier through the valleys of the Ohio and Tennessee rivers. Meanwhile, out of conflict's reach, the Indians in Missouri would undergo a transformation. It was a sublime concept, worthy of Jefferson's best moments of philosophic repose on his Virginia mountaintop. The theory seemed perfect, and the president foresaw the attainment of peace throughout America's interior as a result.

Jefferson's plan for Missouri proved once more how noble hopes for American growth often clashed with cruel circumstance. As with many new areas, any possibility of guided development for Missouri was thwarted by the fact that a sizeable population and even a bit of worldliness and sophistication already existed. Besides Ste. Genevieve, which had been founded as the first enduring community in 1735, and St. Louis, there was Cape Girardeau, established in 1793 by Louis Lorimer, onetime French trader in Ohio who made the mistake of supporting the English in the Revolution before fleeing west. Here was the most American spot at the time of Jefferson's inspired planning, for around "Cape" were many newly arrived Kentuckians who had already begun having a profound impact upon Missouri's history. For these Missouri citizens, the great challenge after 1803 was not selflessly to abandon their places in Missouri to Indian acculturation, but to persuade the new American government to confirm the numerous bequests of land which the Spanish authorities had lavishly distributed in their last moments of rule.

Jefferson soon learned of the vigorous outlook of the Missouri settlers, many of whom had been in the region for a generation. He also discovered that the terms of the purchase required that inhabitants west of the Mississippi must quickly become American citizens. There were also rumors that Napoleon regretted his decision to sell Louisiana and hoped that American delay or blunder would permit him to abrogate the agreement. Sensing how popular the purchase was becoming as news of it spread throughout the United States, Jefferson decided he had no choice but to hasten Congress into session for swift approval of the enormous real estate deal. He sadly laid aside a proposed constitutional amendment which would have indefinitely postponed white settlement and statehood for Missouri.

It seems incredible that Thomas Jefferson even for a moment could imagine it possible to wipe out the results of Missouri's history under France and Spain. No state in its beginnings faced prospects as varied and exciting as Missouri's, whose impetus was not limited to that of the rural frontier. Instead, Missouri at the outset was involved in the efforts of autocratic governments in France and Spain to manage the Mississippi and Missouri river valleys as sources of imperial wealth. The area early won a reputation in European capitals for being a difficult western empire. To the European powers Missouri meant precious metals, especially lead, which proved almost as valuable as silver for a time. Missouri also represented fur pelts, another sort of treasure which trappers, traders, and Indians brought to European agents. In these and other ways, the Missouri region kindled the economic hopes of eighteenth-century Europe, where nations fought for the advantages which overseas possessions were presumed to bring.

The French were first to be interested in Missouri and by 1720 had developed a policy to control traders and governors in the Mississippi valley. Even so, France allowed restrictions, parsimony, and suspicions to handicap her agents for the Missouri region, especially the knowledgeable Jean Baptiste Le Moyne, Sieur de Bienville. For nearly fifty years this man struggled patiently to discover and utilize North America's inland waterways for a France which paid him little heed. Instead, the courage and imagination of many such Frenchmen in America were undone by the waste, ignorance, greed, and folly in Paris.

Just above the future site of St. Louis was the mouth of a mighty river which long puzzled the French. The origin and course of the Missouri were mysteries for decades. From his headquarters in the rising city of New Orleans, Governor Bienville tried repeatedly to learn if this dark and difficult river led to the Orient, or simply to areas where gold, silver, and fur pelts might be found. Since the bureaucrats at the French king's court were clamoring for more wealth from America, Bienville sought help in these matters from one of the most colorful figures in Missouri's history, Etienne Véniard de Bourgmond. Fond of the wilderness and its people, Bourgmond had left Detroit early in the eighteenth century to follow an Indian girl returning to her village on the Missouri River. There, in what became the center of Missouri, Bourgmond thrived for a time. Although his special interest was illicit fur trade, a familiar characteristic of early Missourians, he accepted chores from Governor Bienville in New Orleans. Consequently, by 1714 Bourgmond had paddled up the Missouri River twelve hundred miles in search of the "south sea" and, by 1724, he had established Fort Orleans near the village of the Missouri tribe in present-day Carroll County to thwart anticipated Spanish moves into Missouri from the southwest.

Soon Bourgmond was directed to bring a delegation of Missouri Indians to Paris, where they might see firsthand the glory of France. In July 1725, the French celebrated the arrival of Bourgmond and the Missouri natives. A charming young woman from the Missouri tribe especially captivated Paris. She was baptized in Notre Dame cathedral, beautifully dressed in gold-embroidered garments, designated a Missouri princess, and even called "the Daughter of the Sun." All in all, it was a sensational triumph for the first Missouri girl to visit Paris. The princess eventually married Bourgmond's staff sergeant and returned with her gifts to the tribe along the Missouri River. As for Bourgmond, wearied by his government's indecision and parsimony, he abandoned Missouri life for the delights of a wealthy French widow.

Forty years later, in 1763, French power in Europe and America crumbled from mismanagement just as it attained one of its most important goals. In 1764, a village in Missouri was established in honor of the great medieval figure, Louis IX, king of France in the spectacular thirteenth century and patron saint of the reigning Louis XV. As part of the French enterprise in North America St. Louis was not intended to promote agriculture but trade. The town grew on a handsome site which two visionary Frenchmen selected near the mouth of the Missouri River.

The city's founder, Pierre Liguest Laclede, sprang from an ancient and prominent French family. Apparently trained at the University of Toulouse, Laclede carted some of his most cherished books to New Orleans and then up the Mississippi. When settling in Missouri, he preferred to have around him writings containing Bacon's essays, Locke's views on human understanding, Rousseau's thoughts on the social contract, and the philosophy of Descartes. It was a precedent few would follow. However, Laclede was a man of action as well as reflection, so that he was caught up in French efforts to thrive along the Missouri. In 1763, Gilbert Moxent, a New Orleans merchant, received the right to trade for six years with the Indians on the west bank of the Mississippi. Moxent in turn persuaded Laclede to take the difficult assignment of creating a trading post in Upper Louisiana. As his chief companion, Laclede took his stepson, young Auguste Chouteau, who, as a youth of thirteen, was considered by the custom of the time to have attained his majority.

After these two and their party had settled for the winter at Fort Chartres on the Illinois side of the Mississippi, Laclede took a canoe the short distance to the awesome mouth of the Missouri River. At once attracted to some high ground nearby which overlooked the Mississippi and which had behind it handsome, rolling country, Laclede announced to his followers that he had selected this place to become one of the finest cities in North America. Known for his black piercing eyes, Laclede spoke of seeing extraordinary advantage for a city located so magnificently beside the junction of the two rivers. By February 1764, Laclede put young Chouteau and some workers to felling trees and erecting buildings, making the village of St. Louis a reality. It was an instant if small success, for news soon came that with the close of the Seven Years War, England had won the Illinois land just eastward across the Mississippi. This French setback permitted Laclede to recruit citizens for St. Louis from the uneasy Frenchmen crossing over from nearby Kaskaskia, Cahokia, and Fort Chartres. No one yet knew that the Missouri country itself had been ceded to Spain by France.

Late in 1764, there were perhaps fifty families in the town. They had come to a planned city where everything was carefully chosen and arranged by Laclede. Before the Americans eventually changed all this, citizens walked along the Rue Royal, Rue de l'Eglise, and the Rue des Granges. With such a beginning and with Laclede's books and fine stone house, St. Louis skipped the primitive stage experienced by most of America's frontier hamlets. It never sought to form even a rude democracy, but to be part of an established if unprosperous colonial system: St. Louis was from the outset designed as a commercial center taking advantage of a natural setting, one that Laclede brilliantly foresaw as the crossroads of a continent. It quickly became the focus for westward civilization in North America, a legacy the town would eventually share with the state of Missouri.

Laclede's triumph of imagination at St. Louis was France's last great moment in North America. After 1764, Spain was left holding the slackened bag in the New World once so full of French aspiration for grandeur and wealth. For the balance of the eighteenth century Spain struggled to find a use for the Missouri country, but when she left the area few visible marks of her presence remained. Between 1770 and 1804 probably no more than twenty families who might be called Spanish came to St. Louis. Instead, Spain vacillated, trying to decide if she dared make this countryside a refuge for English-Americans who wished to escape from such places as Ohio, Kentucky, Virginia, and Tennessee. Lured by generous land grants, religious toleration, and the nonexistence of taxes, many Americans did cross into Missouri to become Spaniards. At other times Spain discouraged such immigration, preferring that Missouri be a desolate barrier between her territory and that of England and the United States.

In spite of Spain's confusion, St. Louis and its environs survived, making the town by 1776 the capital of Upper Louisiana. Once the new American nation began pushing into the Ohio River valley after winning independence from England in 1783, Spain grew more agitated. Eager for loyal subjects to make a strong frontier against the United States and England, Spain finally undertook to recruit Americans whom she hoped would be obedient citizens. In attracting such notable pioneers as Daniel Boone, Moses Austin, and George Morgan, founder of the village of New Madrid, Spain expected to have dutiful servants of the crown. She accepted even Protestants as residents of Missouri if they subscribed to the loyalty oath. As part of her strategy for peopling Missouri, Spain used such a soldier of fortune as the controversial American, James Wilkinson. He seemed willing to act not only as Madrid's agent in encouraging Kentuckians to enter Missouri, but also possibly to tempt Kentucky over to the Spanish flag.

Until 1795 most settlers in the Missouri region were Frenchmen from Canada and the Mississippi's east bank. Then Spain signed the treaty which opened the Mississippi River to American trade, and Missouri immigration immediately increased. Thereafter, nearly all the newcomers were Americans drawn by the two great assets Spanish rule had to offer—free land and no taxes. Those Americans who crossed into Missouri found unfamiliar values and institutions, for citizens of St. Louis, Ste. Genevieve, New Madrid, and Cape Girardeau knew nothing, for example, of jury duty. Under traditions and laws from France and Spain, there were no elections, and the spirit of mercantilism prevailed, permitting leadership to rest with businessmen, especially fur traders and mine operators. There was a charming, unhurried quality about life inherited from the French which often struck the compulsive Americans as indolence. The fact that nearly everyone claimed to be a Roman Catholic added to the strangeness felt by most newcomers from the United States. However, when they emigrated to Missouri late in the 1790s, men such as Daniel Boone and Moses Austin knew they were abandoning their nationality to become subjects of the Spanish monarch.

For a brief time, Missouri was the center of power politics with global implications. In the area surrounding St. Louis Spain contemplated making a stand against European and New World rivals as she sought to refashion her own strength in two hemispheres. Presently, however, the Madrid government recognized that its success in North America was neither better nor less expensive than France's had been. By secret treaty Spain returned the region, including Missouri, to France in 1800, allowing France under Napoleon to entertain brief dreams of renewing glory in North America. Then Napoleon bowed to reality. Instead of sending French legions to make Missouri a footstool for his empire, the French leader startled President Jefferson's envoys in 1803 by offering them the vast reaches along the Mississippi and Missouri rivers for $15 million.

When Thomas Jefferson's emissaries arrived in St. Louis, citizens of that town had only recently learned of their transfer from France to the United States. With French, Spanish, and American backgrounds, most residents in Missouri had simply been trying to prosper together. For them, distant governments, whether in Paris, Madrid, or Washington, were watched in hope of commercial or military aid or in fear of bureaucratic, ignorant hindrances. By 1804, many of those residing in the vicinity of St. Louis were American in origin. Yet these colonists had made no effort to overthrow their monarch and no popular machination impelled the Missouri region into the United States empire. Since most Missourians, especially persons like Auguste Chouteau who had lived under three flags, were interested in thriving, they watched with mixed feelings as the Stars and Stripes replaced the flags of Spain and France on 10 March 1804. Events did not keep them waiting long.

Soon, the population around St. Louis and beyond increased rapidly and life became more rewarding and complicated—changes that resulted from President Jefferson's second, and this time highly successful, personal involvement in the early story of Missouri. Quickly putting aside his disappointment in making Missouri an Indian kingdom, Jefferson renewed his longstanding interest in learning about the land stretching beyond the Mississippi. To satisfy his and the nation's curiosity, he launched one of the most famous explorations in the history of discovery. It was at the order of an eager president that Meriwether Lewis and William Clark began their famed trip along the Missouri River. The Lewis and Clark expedition from 1804 to 1806 had many marvelous results, not the least of which was a ripening of America's appreciation of the Missouri region and the tempting of many new settlers into the countryside beyond St. Louis. The town saw the explorers depart, expecting them to return with confirmation that St. Louis marked the start of the fabled route to the Pacific and thus to the Orient.

Jefferson wanted Lewis and Clark to undertake a task greater than that of simply proving the region would support a fabulous amount of trade through St. Louis. The expedition left the town with instructions to find the mouth of the Columbia River, which

Capt. Robert Gray had discovered in 1792. Beyond this was Jefferson's determination to make as many useful Indian contacts as possible and to acquire the information needed to assure a permanent trade in the Northwest. Furthermore, Jefferson expected Lewis and Clark to dispel a general ignorance about the large interior on the map of North America. The expedition responded handsomely to its tasks, leaving Missouri greatly indebted to it. Because of the astonishing physical and emotional courage of Lewis and Clark, all the world soon learned that the little settlements in Missouri stood as gatekeepers to new natural wealth of indescribable variety and abundance. The restless curiosity of Thomas Jefferson made Missouri and its marvelous river the key to America's western kingdom. It was precisely the result Jefferson had first wanted to avoid.

Jefferson and his successor as president, James Madison, turned to Lewis and Clark in governing some of the Missouri countryside with results that were less happy than those of the great expedition. Meriwether Lewis became territorial governor of Missouri in 1807, succeeding Jefferson's earlier choice, the troublesome James Wilkinson. Lewis was well-educated and sophisticated, but also mercurial and moody. He appeared to feel personally the difficulties with the Indians in the region as well as the frustrations of keeping in touch with the distant federal capital. To many early Missourians, Governor Lewis seemed unsympathetic with the impatient traders and overly concerned with Indian rights. Having launched a judicial system in the territory and having encouraged the first newspaper west of the Mississippi, both major achievements, a despondent Lewis decided in 1809 to travel to Washington and attempt to dispel confusion over his personal expenditures. Evidently his courage bowed to his melancholia, for in western Tennessee Meriwether Lewis died, an apparent suicide.

A happier spirit and career belonged to William Clark. With Jefferson and Lewis, he shared a profound regard for the Indians and their rights. Clark's personality and talents as a frontiersman were such that the Indians, in turn, admired and trusted him. To the tribes in Missouri, Clark was known as the Red Headed Chief. While most of his career was devoted to managing Indian affairs, William Clark did serve as territorial governor from 1813 to 1820. When the state elected its first executive in 1820, however, Clark was defeated decisively by Alexander McNair, making it evident that few Missouri voters shared Clark's regard for the Indians or admired his concessions to them. In addition, Clark was harmed by some increasingly unpopular political alliances as well as by his absence from the state in 1820 because of his wife's illness in Virginia. Despite this reversal, however, Clark continued to serve the region, dying in 1838 in St. Louis, nearly a generation after his patience and wisdom contributed decisively to concluding Indian disputes in Missouri.

During William Clark's long tenure as territorial governor, Missouri proved to be a difficult child in the American empire. The difficulty sprang in part from the fact the youngster was adopted, bringing problems from previous families. Between 1804 and 1815 Washington received many formal and informal pleas from Missourians for aid or redress. Accustomed to Spanish governance which was simple and near at hand, Missouri found the federalism of the United States exasperatingly different. Gov. Meriwether Lewis had complained bitterly that efforts to get advice from his superiors in the District of Columbia usually entailed two months. Even so, Governor Lewis and his successors faced problems in the Missouri region that more direct consultation with Washington might not have helped.

For example, the vital fur trade was undependable, requiring clearer governmental support in the opinion of many merchants and trappers. Even more exasperating was the grief brought by the land titles Spain had awarded to numerous Missourians, for the validity of many grants were thrown into doubt because the United States hesitated to accept them. Another problem was the relentless rumor that the Indians were out for blood and plunder, increasing the demand for a harsh policy toward the Indians instead of the courtesy and concern shown by William Clark and other federal agents. None of these hazards in early Missouri was aided by the intense suspicion and actual dislike which arose in some areas between the older French settlers and the newer Americans.

Such issues were made doubly exasperating because of confusing information and alarming rumors inherited from Jefferson's administration, for while the president's initial determination to block white settlement in Missouri had been discarded, it lingered as a fertile source for disquiet. Stories abounded in Missouri hamlets that white men would be moved to the Illinois country, leaving red men in charge of the Missouri valley. Added to this were reports that Congress planned to free all slaves in the region purchased from France. Missouri was full of misgiving, encouraging an interest in rumors about plans to detach the region for a happy reunion with Spain. Former Vice-President Aaron Burr, the man who had slain Alexander Hamilton in a duel, appeared in the territory early in 1807, and tales spread that he and his cohort, Gov. James Wilkinson, were about to lead Missouri to a more comfortable harbor out of the Union.

The effect of these rumors was fleeting compared to the long furor over the land claims of numerous Missourians. Farmers and speculators alike became convinced that Spain's casual land grants would be disallowed on a massive scale by the United States, whose government seemed to believe that behind every Missouri bush lurked a thief intent on depriving America of land now its to sell. While some speculators doubtless thrived by using bits of paper hurriedly distributed by departing Spanish officials, there were many distressing instances of individuals caught between the territory and the nation.

The difficulties of Daniel Boone were especially interesting. After Kentucky courts declared his land claims there invalid, the venerable woodsman followed his sons across the Mississippi. Boone arrived in Missouri in 1798, encouraged by Spanish officials who awarded him land equaling 8,500 acres. In 1800, Boone was named syndic or commandant of the Femme Osage district along the Missouri River somewhat southwest of St. Louis. Consequently, he failed to take steps required to confirm his land concession, later claiming that Spanish authorities told him these were unnecessary because he was a syndic. By 1807, Boone and numerous other alarmed citizens were appearing before a United States board of land commissioners to ask confirmation of their land claims. Feelings ran high, so much so that on one occasion an indignant claimant interrupted the commissioners' proceedings in order to beat one member with a cane.

When his plea was rejected, Boone joined more than 2,000 other persons whose claims were set aside for such reasons as lack of proper registration, unduly large size, belated survey, or erroneous signatures. Boone's national reputation brought him a temporary reprieve when Congress saluted his service to the nation by awarding him title to a tenth of his Spanish claim through special legislation in 1814. Alas, however, for Boone. His creditors back in old "Kaintuck" heard of his good fortune and hastened to Missouri to collect, so that the pathfinder's Spanish grant never comforted his declining years. For a time it seemed that all claims dated after 1800 would be invalid. The rising public clamor produced a more liberal policy after 1814; although the dispute over land lingered until after the Civil War. Many of Missouri's early political and social rifts were the result of land policy, thereby giving Missourians further reason to develop their famous cautiousness.

The Spanish grants were scarcely the sole cause of land dispute. Other complications came after southeastern Missouri around New Madrid was devastated by massive earthquakes, involving tremors during the winter of 1811–1812 which exceeded in severity the San Francisco quake of 1906. Among the vibrations, some sensed as far away as New Orleans, Detroit, Boston, and the District of Columbia, was the one of 7 February 1812, which reportedly was most severe. It hurled the Mississippi River to astounding heights while the land was transformed, leaving lakes where forests once grew, and wide areas containing fields and orchards were rent by great chasms. Because settlements were so scattered, few citizens were injured. However, many were outraged by the controversy over the certificates for new land which Congress eventually issued to victims in exchange for their devastated property. For years refugees from the quake struggled to get proper acknowledgment for their land certificates but often had to contend with unscrupulous speculators and a hesitant government. The result was another cause for bitterness and a negative view of society among Missourians.

After 1815, when the second war with England concluded and the uncertainty over Indians and land ownership diminished, the population of Missouri Territory increased even more rapidly. In 1818, the federal government at last felt confident enough to allow public land to go on sale. Two years later, the territory claimed to have 56,000 white inhabitants, plus nearly 10,000 slaves and perhaps 375 free blacks. Towns and counties grew steadily beyond St. Louis, as well as along the Mississippi, so that settlement began to flourish as far west as the future border county of Jackson at the great bend of the Missouri River, where stood Fort Osage, an important post for Indian relations. Between St. Louis and Fort Osage were the villages of Franklin, Boonville, and Lexington as well as the popular Boonslick region which the sons of Daniel Boone had made so attractive. Some of those who did not settle along the river's westward course instead moved northward into the Salt River country. South of the Missouri River an enthusiasm for lead mining brought both miners and farmers into Washington, Jefferson, and Madison counties, three units which were created before Missouri became a state.

The earliest group of counties to be organized had names reflecting the French and Spanish influences. In 1812, Cape Girardeau, New Madrid, St. Charles, St. Louis, and Ste. Genevieve counties were created. After 1818, counties were given such American names as Franklin, Lincoln, Pike, Wayne, Ray, Montgomery, Cooper, and Boone. Eventually there would be 114 counties and the independent city of St. Louis, making a decentralized scheme of government which the state has never ceased to cherish. As the counties appeared, the towns in the territory flourished, and the population of St. Louis more than doubled between 1815 and 1821. Communities such as Ste. Genevieve, St. Charles, and Franklin also prospered.

From this swelling but apprehensive populace went numerous petitions and memorials to Congress on matters such as land, government, Indians, and statehood. It was on the last topic that Missourians could put aside their many disagreements, for despite the presence in Washington after 1816 of John Scott, who ably served Missouri as territorial delegate, most of his constituents believed their problems would never be resolved until Missouri became a state. By 1818 the call for statehood so dominated public discourse that when the movement encountered sensational congressional delays, Missourians were drawn together in anger and suspicion toward the United States.

The admission of Missouri to the Union caused one of America's most famous political conflicts. Never before or since did a request for statehood create such an outcry, so that in arguing over Missouri many Americans actually saw the specter of disunion. Three sessions of Congress, between 1818 and 1821, considered the issue before finally admitting Missouri. The agreement ultimately reached in 1820 was known to succeeding generations as the Missouri Compromise, an understanding among the sections of the nation which lasted until, battered and broken, it collapsed in 1854. The chief issue raised by Missouri's request for statehood was not her readiness for admission, but whether slavery should move further into the Louisiana Purchase country. Congress's answer to this concern, reached only after a storm had spread far beyond the halls of the Capitol, was relatively simple. Missouri entered the Union without restriction, which meant that slavery would continue in the state. Votes for this proviso became possible when the portion of Massachusetts known as Maine asked Congress to make it a free state. This "one and one" arrangement seemed to preserve a numerical and political balance in the Union between slave and free states.

However, the most extraordinary and for many the most embarrassing part of the Missouri Compromise was making the southern boundary of Missouri—the famed 36°30' line—a division between bondage and liberty in the Louisiana Purchase region. Congress decreed that except for Missouri, slavery was prohibited north of the 36°30' latitude. Many federal representatives and senators, exhausted from the long and tense debates, consoled themselves that by permitting this demarcation between freedom and slavery, they had preserved the American experiment in democracy. They reasoned that time eventually

would bring the wisdom for a final, peaceable solution to the
slavery issue. Besides, most individuals believed that Missouri
would be the last state to seek admission for a generation. They
were nearly right, since fifteen years passed before Arkansas
asked to become a state.

The Missouri Compromise was not easily attained. For a time
it appeared that no harmonious agreement was possible over
Missouri's statehood. Since the United States had in 1787 forbidden Negro bondage in the lands above the Ohio River, many
congressmen thirty years later contended that a similar prohibition should be placed upon the region beyond the Mississippi
River. In Congress, in Missouri, and across the nation, the line
over Missouri's admission was drawn between restrictionists,
which meant those who were determined to confine slavery to
the old area east of the Mississippi, and those who favored slavery by opposing any restriction.

Out of the debates emerged the first significant claims that
slavery was an actual good. From the other side came talk of the
need somehow to rid the nation of black bondage. The furor
was by no means confined to Congress. In North and South,
journalists, clergymen, orators, members of grand juries, atten-
dants at public meetings, and speakers at banquets all contributed to the debate over what Missouri's future meant for
America. An important feature of the controversy was the belief
that the Missouri question allowed the United States a chance to
let morality shape its policy. If slavery in Missouri were to be
terminated and the Louisiana region closed to the evil, many
northerners argued that the nation would have repaid the debt
for ever having permitted black bondage to begin. With slavery
excluded from Missouri, they predicted it would ultimately dis-
appear everywhere. Opponents of this view also claimed to
embrace moral principles. For them an unrestricted Missouri
symbolized the superior authority of the states, the cornerstone
of the Union in their minds.

As the debate wore on, Missouri citizens generally agreed
that from both principle and the spirit of the Louisiana Purchase
treaty, they deserved unconditional statehood. They were indignant at the thought of any restriction. For Congress to hesitate

only further enraged territorial sentiment, leading to widespread talk among Missourians of a Washington conspiracy to upset their rightful place in the Union. Missouri orators and grand juries were therefore careful to eulogize sacred property rights and state equality. Generally, the territory took the position that she was an injured, innocent party and determined that she would fight for the noble American ideals of an untrammeled statehood, an ideal which evidently most of America had forgotten. Emboldened toastmakers at territorial banquets proclaimed that Missourians would gladly shed blood to defend their rights. The effect of all this on Missouri was to submerge the issue of slavery, leaving citizens the morally easier argument for state prerogatives. In fact, the importation of slaves into Missouri had proceeded more slowly than had been anticipated. As a result the issue of slavery became in Missouri more important as a symbolic device than as an economic practice.

Those who watched the congressional tumult from faraway Missouri believed that the motives hindering their statehood were rooted in fears that Missouri's notable location and potential wealth would permit her to take an early commanding position in the Union. It was difficult for many in St. Louis, in the Boonslick region, or elsewhere in Missouri to recognize that her admission to the Union brought the nation an important choice between embracing or evading principle. It was a choice which was deferred, however, when a national majority decided that the Union's preservation was a principle superior to that of restricting slavery. Most combatants subsided, telling themselves that it was better to make the fight for principle within the Union than through dismemberment. The adjudication of issues raised by Missouri's admission may have left few persons satisfied, but it relieved the nation from long dispute and calls for disunion.

While the terms of the famous compromise were agreed upon in 1820, the quarrel again broke loose later that year. A disgruntled Missouri, determined to have the final word, prepared a constitution which required the general assembly to establish statutes banning free blacks from entering the new state. When this constitution was submitted to Congress, in accord with final procedures for admitting states, the shout arose that Missouri was deliberately insulting the United States. Consequently, many antislave congressmen took the new opportunity to insist that Missouri's admission be delayed until she consented to the gradual abolition of slavery. This put Missouri and the United States at loggerheads in the winter of 1820–1821, with the compromise evidently spoiled. However, a face-saving arrangement was devised by Henry Clay, the great pacifier from Kentucky. Sensing that emotions were cooling both in Congress and in Missouri, Clay arranged for admission to be completed when Missouri would formally agree to forbid legislation which would deprive citizens from other states of rights bestowed by the national constitution. Missouri complied, although in ill humor. On 10 August 1821, President James Monroe proclaimed that the Union had its twenty-fourth state.

The newcomer still was determined to have the last word, however. After waiting a brief interval, the Missouri legislature brazenly approved statutes keeping free blacks outside the state. This step may have helped some Missourians believe their state was not to be trifled with, but the long view must consider it one of Missouri's most disgraceful moments. Young Missouri, full of pride, had actually behaved as a state for a year before her painful admission was confirmed. On 19 July 1820, members of the Missouri constitutional convention in St. Louis had adopted their own handiwork, claiming it must take effect at once. In the late summer, the election of a congressman, a governor, and general assembly members took place. By October 1820, two United States senators had been chosen and Missouri stood ready to be active in the Union, furious at the delay.

In this controversial manner Missouri became part of the nation's history. She kept an important role until 1875. By the time of her statehood travelers and writers were already praising Missouri's natural wealth and strategic location. Her principal city was called the Memphis of the American Nile. Taking great pride in this natural legacy, Missourians in 1820 liked to say that pioneers such as Bourgmond, Laclede, Lewis, Clark, and the Boones had uncovered a great physical empire over which the state must now preside. Furthermore, amid the excitement over statehood, Daniel Boone had died. This sad event was taken by Missourians as a solemn indication that their state must now put the pioneer phase of her life behind her and begin a mature and mighty career in the nation.

3

Nature's Legacy

*Y*OUNG as Missouri may have been within the United States in 1821, her natural prowess on the North American continent had already brought her admiration and attention. With a colorful career behind her as participant in the western dreams of France, Spain, and the United States, Missouri seemed both gateway to and mistress of a vast new land. Geopolitics would, in fact, make Missouri one of the dominant states in American history before the Civil War. By 1820, the legend about Daniel Boone, the writings of Jedediah Morse (America's first geographer), the exploits of Lewis and Clark, the tales about trappers and traders, and the accumulation of books by western travelers had kept the nation fascinated with Missouri. This attention was especially flattering in an era before technology tempted men to take the forces of nature less seriously.

Missouri was said to have been particularly blessed by nature. During the 1820s, America talked of an old and a new West, with some persons ever mentioning Missouri as a second Eden. Thomas Jefferson was by no means the only individual who envisoned the Missouri region as an unspoiled area where a second phase of American development might be allowed to build on the lessons of experience. Missouri opened into a second America, as if the Mississippi River divided the nation into two great communities, with the newer portion being much grander and more promising than the eastern region—the mountains and rivers in the East looked puny beside those of the West. In a sense the new state seemed to be located on the edges of two American civilizations that joined at the Mississippi.

If Missouri and her mighty river were a broad avenue into another America, then the new state and her thriving city, St. Louis, became the portal or anchor for distant realms of incalculable wealth. This was Missouri's second natural advantage, reflecting the ancient dreams of passage to the Orient. Missourians hoped their state would be the eastern terminus of such a route. They saw the route as one that would mean a new posture for the entire Republic: through Missouri, America would turn to face far across the Pacific and would escape the old dependence upon the Atlantic Ocean and Europe. Anticipations of the riches to be carried across a Missouri located between two worlds eventually encouraged transcontinental railroading. When this finally happened, Missouri suffered an ironical blow, since railroads disregarded nature's traditional paths.

A youthful Missouri thus stood as a second Eden, as gateway and guardian for a wondrous new America and distant wealth. The prospect obviously appealed to the nation's greatest orator, Daniel Webster, who confessed his awe at Missouri's natural eminence. Speaking in St. Louis in 1837, Webster acknowledged that the nation had not yet fully appreciated what he called an infant Hercules. According to the Massachusetts senator, Missouri had more mineral and agricultural wealth than any other area on earth. A few years later, Ralph Waldo Emerson was barely less eloquent when he said that the meeting of the Missouri River with the Mississippi was the world's greatest crossroad. Such wide interest in her natural wealth and prominence encouraged Missourians to believe in their state's universal strength, for who could deny that nature had dealt generously with the state, leaving handsome bequests of marvelous land, river valleys, forests, mineral deposits, and helpful weather? So much was said about Missouri's possessing all resources needed for a glorious life that a smugness arose among the citizens. It remained popular even in the last half of the twentieth century for adults and school children alike to assert that if the rest of the universe fell away, Missouri would get on very nicely.

Certainly if completeness was the measure, nature intended Missouri as another Eden. It is not surprising that an early Missouri college, one founded by German immigrants, was named Eden Seminary. The variety of the state's geography and resources hinted at a wholeness worthy of the original Paradise. She had vast woodlands, including what would become two national forests. In the southeastern lowland, known as the boot heel region, where Missouri would remain very southern, cotton would flourish, while extensive prairie land far to the northwest would make Missouri a major cattle producer. Between these extremes cereals, hemp, tobacco, dairy industry, poultry, and mining of several varieties would thrive, as well as a fascination with trade which eventually established two of America's major cities on Missouri's borders. There was room for all of this to develop, for Missouri was a large state with nearly 70,000 square miles. Within this extent, of course, lay Missouri's wondrous river system, which her citizens especially cherished. Missourians knew from the beginning how important the Mississippi and Missouri rivers had made their state. They contended that the Missouri River was the longest and most powerful stream in the world, leaving the Mississippi its tributary. After all, the Missouri drew from an area of 530,000 square miles, while to its juncture with the Missouri the Mississippi drained only 171,000 square miles of countryside.

Regardless of perspective, the meeting place of the Missouri and Mississippi rivers was one of the earth's most momentous sites. For Missouri it meant strength and pride until technology overcame the ancient primacy of water civilization. Missouri never was the same after the river gods were deposed. As the rivers retreated before rail, motor, and air travel, Missouri's population, relative wealth, and political significance also diminished. However, the legacy of water was not forsaken by the people of Missouri, and even now, after 150 years of statehood and a century after the railroad arrived, Missourians still consider rivers important. Rivers always referred to watercourses other than the powerful Missouri and the Mississippi. In the northwestern quarter the Platte and Grand rivers dominated, while toward the north central and northeast, the Chariton and Salt rivers were important. Through the southwestern quarter of the state came the Osage River, which emptied into the Missouri near the mouth of the Gasconade, flowing northward out of the Ozark Hills and springs. Then, below St. Louis, from the west, ran the Meramec River which coursed for nearly 250 miles. In southern Missouri was the great trio, the Current, the Black, and the St. Francis rivers. Finally, the White River flowed along Missouri's southern border toward the west, the principal stream of the Ozark country made famous by Harold Bell Wright.

Missouri's natural glory was first beheld from the rivers. The pioneers, whether farmers or traders, joined the rivermen in thinking of Missouri as land lying along marvelous, even awesome river pathways. Early letters and books about the Missouri country stressed the rivers as a matter of course. One of these writers, Henry M. Brackenridge, went up the Missouri with the famed trader, Manuel Lisa, in 1811. They made quite a pair after Brackenridge became accustomed to life on a flatboat powered by men and sail. When the two were not reading aloud together from Cervantes, Brackenridge wrote about the Missouri River and the land along its banks in his journal, which was later published. His pages captured some of the jubilation over what he saw, as when he wrote of the area around the Osage River: "The beauty and fertility of the surrounding country cannot be surpassed." Everywhere, glorious land seemed "almost boundless," allowing Brackenridge to announce that Missouri was "capable of producing whatever may administer to the convenience or luxury of man; rich in minerals, fertile in soil, and favorably situated for commerce and manufacture." He found it difficult to speak of Missouri except as "delightful," "beautiful," "charming," and "not to be surpassed." [1]

1. Henry Marie Brackenridge, *Journal of a Voyage Up the River Missouri,* as reprinted in Reuben Gold Thwaites, *Early Western Travels,* 32 vols. (Cleveland: A. H. Clark, 1904), 6. See especially pp. 27, 44–46, 160–163.

Another author, Henry R. Schoolcraft, left the rivers in 1818 to tramp through Missouri's southeastern wilderness. Occasionally he found a cabin of a farmer or trader, but mostly Schoolcraft was seeing an unspoiled country which he felt would have enormous appeal for painters. His language was similar to Brackenridge's as he wrote of "the face of nature in its wildest aspect of rocky grandeur." Giving attention to the mineral riches in the Meramec River valley and the Current River area, Schoolcraft exclaimed over a quantity of materials beyond that found anywhere else in America, with lead deposits, especially, exceeding those "which the United States, or any mining district of Europe or America affords." In fact, when Schoolcraft published the story of his Missouri travels, he added a poem called "Transallegania, or The Groans of Missouri." Here the distress of all the metals at seeing Missouri discovered and populated took the form of the New Madrid earthquake:

> So great was the tumult, confusion, and groans
> Such horrors arose from the clashing of stones.[2]

While travelers such as Brackenridge and Schoolcraft drew impressive portraits of Missouri's natural glory, Europe was also hearing about the wealth of this new state. In 1829, a German physician and lawyer, Gottfried Duden, offered his fellow countrymen a *Report on a Journey to the Western States of America and a Stay of Several Years along the Missouri*. From 1824 to 1827 Duden resided in the Femme Osage district, which the Boones had made famous. Generally considered to be the book most influencing German migration to America, Duden's volume praised the natural wealth as early Missourians saw it. He had the imagination of a physiocrat, certain that the rural, agrarian existence was ennobling and happy, so that for him Missouri had a Garden of Eden charm. His *Report* was criticized by many who found life in Missouri more difficult than Duden implied, largely because many readers were so enchanted with Duden's ecstatic accounts of Missouri's wonders

2. Henry R. Schoolcraft, *Journal of a Tour into the Interior of Missouri and Arkansaw* (London: R. Phillips, 1821), especially pp. 3, 10–11, 90.

that they failed to heed carefully his sobering counsel on diseases, loneliness, and clearing land. Duden's views drew serious consideration, for he came to Missouri with an inquiring mind, determined to see the state for himself since available descriptions had left him unsatisfied. No one such as Duden, accustomed to the physical limitations imposed by time and populace upon Europe, could quite remain dispassionate on seeing how lavishly nature had graced Missouri. Duden was especially impressed with Missouri's river system which he claimed was unequaled in the world. Although Warren County's beauty so overwhelmed him that he insisted he could not do it justice by description, Duden nevertheless went on to rapturous talk of the dense forests, the grapevines (twelve inches thick), and the prodigiously fertile soil.

However, it took a migrant New England clergyman and Harvard College alumnus to picture best the rich legacy Missouri had from nature's hand. The Rev. Timothy Flint's famed *Recollections of the Last Ten Years* became a widely read classic. Published in 1826, it emphasized years Flint and his family spent in the Missouri River village of St. Charles. Flint believed no one could be unmoved who saw this "river which rises in vast and nameless mountains, and runs at one time through deep forests, and then through grassy plains, between three and four thousand miles before it arrives here." It was a river "more fierce and unsparing in its wrath" than the Mississippi, which Flint also watched awestruck. As for the Missouri countryside, Flint said it was unnecessary "to be very young or very romantic, in order to have dreams steal over the mind, of spending an Arcadian life in these remote plains, which just begin to be vexed with the plough, far removed from the haunts of wealth and fashion, in the midst of rustic plenty, and of this beautiful nature."

Flint was moved even to admire Missouri's citizens, bringing him to announce that "there is kindness and sympathy with distress, and christian feeling, in the prairies of Missouri," a noble setting where people were far from "ignorant and barbarous." Flint discovered "generous hearts" and "elevated minds every where," strongly implying that nature produced better men as well as superior plants, minerals, trees, and animals in Missouri. There, said Flint, nature has decreed that "any person, able and disposed to labour, is forever freed from the apprehension of poverty." He rejected the belief that such abundance would breed sloth. In Missouri, "a man of good principles and habits will find useful and happy employment for all that time, which the wants of actual subsistence do not require." Flint's Adam in this Eden found a rich and full life, thanks to nature's bounty and a virtuous outlook. For Flint the Missouri River's "everlasting roll" seemed to promise an eternal setting for America's fulfillment.[3]

In Flint's and Duden's day many new Missourians arrived determined to wring from the natural legacy their own immediate achievement. But Missouri was much like any other frontier, so that newcomers found diligence, fortitude, energy, and imagination were required in order to receive nature's blessing. Although legend may hint that men in early Missouri were of a superior if not superhuman stamp, the reality was far different. Failure, misery, poverty, and imprudence, as well as violence and corruption, were qualities and conditions brought into the Missouri Eden. Curiously, an old Missouri expression for a man's failure was to be "up Salt River," a term recalling the futile efforts of local citizens, including Sam Clemens's father, to improve navigation on Salt River. In Missouri nature's bounty could also be nature's mockery.

Somber possibilities were not unknown as early citizens came to enlarge Missouri's role in American history. The career of Moses Austin illustrated what happened to some who believed Missouri would be America's mineral colossus. Just as Frenchmen and Spaniards had listened earlier to descriptions of the precious metal supposedly found everywhere in Upper Louisiana, so Moses Austin heeded the prospects for lead in Missouri. Arriving in 1798 to become one of the state's significant figures, Austin was an experienced miner who cautiously left Virginia to enter Spanish Missouri to find the truth about nature's achievement. Initially Austin was not disappointed. In the

---

3. Timothy Flint, *Recollections of the Last Ten Years* (Boston: Cummings, Hilliard, 1826), pp. 85, 120–124, 188, 191, 220, 230, 246, 289–291.

area west of Ste. Genevieve he saw galena deposits near the earth's surface which he believed surpassed the best lead ore in America or England. Thereupon, Austin introduced mature mining to Missouri, whereas previously, the technique involved a pathetic scratching at surface deposits with a highly inefficient smelting method which lost about two-thirds of the lead. Using his handsome land grant around Mine à Breton, Austin soon displayed a mastery over Missouri's minerals. He sank the first significant mine shaft in the region; he produced shot, cannonballs, and sheet lead; and he created a reverberating furnace which had a smelting process twice as efficient as any used previously. He also established a sawmill and a flour mill.

Unfortunately, the need for lead proved neither enormous nor persistent. While Missouri had the world's largest deposit of galena and steadily served as the leading producer of lead, the benefits of such attainment were easily exaggerated. By 1815, Austin's lead business was diminishing while his troubles as a St. Louis banking participant were growing. Eager for yet another start, Austin began thinking about colonizing Texas with Missourians. Once again he ventured into Spanish country and went in 1820 to San Antonio, where he discovered that Texas and Mexico had become independent of Spain. Mexico encouraged Austin's plan to bring 300 of his Missouri neighbors to yet another Eden, but the old pioneer never realized his hope. He died in 1821 soon after an exhausting winter trip back to Missouri. He left to his talented son, Stephen F. Austin, a plea that the Texas colony proceed. Soon Stephen Austin's success in creating a second Missouri provided the first evidence of how the state would mother the West.

Leaving his father buried in Missouri, Stephen Austin took up his father's grant of thousands of Texas acres and brought with him many Missourians. In fact, most of the 300 families who became the first American Texans belonged to the Austin colony. He found little difficulty in attracting colonists, for the Austins were well known in Missouri Territory, since Moses had greatly enhanced its wealth and Stephen had served in its territorial legislature. Two other Missourians, Greene C. DeWitt and James Kerr, successfully emulated Stephen Austin, helping to build the colony in Texas and to develop it as a Missouri province. These colonists brought an ingrained Missouri skepticism about things Spanish, a quality which helped move Texas toward becoming an independent republic by 1836. In this way the story of Texas's beginning was closely related to economic disappointments in Missouri, especially in mining and banking. The Austins had found the mineral development in Missouri less than they had anticipated. Such was to be the experience of the state as a whole.

After the Civil War, there were some spectacular revivals of mining zeal in Missouri. One of the most colorful was in the southwest near Joplin where by 1872 zinc was found in an abundance exceeding that of lead. For a time this discovery produced the growth and violence usually associated with gold rush days. Meanwhile, enthusiasts in St. Louis were trying with little success to persuade America to acclaim Missouri the "Iron Mountain State." Nevertheless, despite her supplies of iron and coal, Missouri never became a leading mineral state, as measured by the value of annual production. Compared to the Minnesota, Michigan, Pennsylvania, and New York achievements, Missouri lagged well behind although not far enough to escape the strip mining and forest decimation which brought tragic scars of brutality against nature's seemingly limitless bounty.

As appealing as mining to many persons in Moses Austin's day was the likelihood that Missouri would be the center for North America's fur trade. One of the Missourians who best understood the challenge of the fur industry was Manuel Lisa, who lived much of his life struggling up the Missouri River on keelboats to outdistance the British in contacting the Indian and white trappers. Lisa dreamed as early as 1807 of making the Northwest a source of great wealth for Missouri and America; he believed the British must be shown that the United States was serious about using the Louisiana Purchase. Above all, however, Lisa concentrated on making the upper Missouri country a marvelous estate for St. Louis. Toward that end he had his men wandering the upper ranges of the Rockies while he became the acknowledged master of Missouri River travel as well as of trade for the beaver pelt. Lisa had the capacity to see far beyond the keelboats piled high with furs returning to St. Louis. Unfortunately his business colleagues were interested only in pelts and hides, no matter how they were secured. While several St. Louis firms, especially the Missouri Fur Company, needed Lisa's wisdom and energy, they found his large vision a handicap.

Manuel Lisa considered the fur trade simply a means of opening the natural miracle of the vast region bound to Missouri by the great river. He believed that enterprise along the river should begin with permanent accord with the Indian tribes. Tirelessly but in futility Lisa tried to persuade his St. Louis brethren that investments in Indian friendship, initially expensive in time and gifts, would yield handsome dividends. The difficulty was that establishing cordiality with the Indians required the use of time and gifts which threatened the profits of the struggling St. Louis fur business. Lisa's painstaking attitude toward Indians grew from his insistence that the Missouri country was a region to be won slowly and knowledgeably. By learning, by friendship and partnership with the Indians, by creating trading posts as centers for settlement, and by intense competition with the British trading system, Lisa sought to use nature's legacy wisely.

Lisa's prowess on the river became a legend. In a span of thirteen years, he went up the Missouri at least twelve times, often reaching the Mandan village, 1,500 miles from his rarely used home in St. Louis. Only William Clark drew as much genuine comradeship and respect from the Indians as did Lisa, who with his wife from the Omaha tribe had two children. Toward them Lisa displayed great concern even after he later married a woman from a prominent St. Louis family. This wife, Mary Hempstead Keeney Lisa, shared her husband's philosophy and accompanied him on his last trip upriver in 1819, thereby becoming the first white woman to ascend the Missouri. Mrs. Lisa was so eager for amity with the Indians that somehow she sat through the finest of their tributes, a banquet featuring roast dog. With Lisa's death in 1820 departed his concept of an orderly bond between St. Louis and the magnificent West. The fur trade carried on after Lisa, but without vision. Missouri soon had to share the fur enterprise, so that Lisa's haunts were trapped out by 1840, leaving a heritage of bitterness with the Indians and an example of man's profligate claims upon nature's bounty.

Another attempt to capitalize on Missouri's natural advantages began with William Becknell, who mixed luck, ingenuity, and courage to become father of the Santa Fe Trail. Long before Becknell's achievement in 1822, Missourians knew of the fabled area in the Southwest and of Spain's determination to keep Americans out of those provinces. It was a helpful coincidence, therefore, that when Missouri entered the federal Union, Mexico herself was throwing off Spanish rule to become a republic. In late summer of 1821, none of this was known to Becknell, a merchant in the bustling town of Franklin, located in the middle of the state along the Missouri River. Leading a group of traders and trappers toward the Rocky Mountains for commerce with the Indians, Becknell was astonished to encounter Mexicans who were cordial rather than antagonistic. From this meeting Becknell learned that the country around Santa Fe had become eager for trade with America.

The Franklin merchant hastened with his small stock of goods to Santa Fe, arriving there on 16 November 1821. Not only was he warmly welcomed, but the Mexicans exchanged silver bullion for Becknell's paltry Indian supplies. With this happy occasion, the exciting days of America's first road across the great West began. It fired ideas that Missouri was a step closer toward being America's port of commerce with the Orient. Becknell returned to Franklin in January 1822 with his saddlebags filled with Mexican silver dollars. Thereupon Franklin strove mightily to become the terminus for United States commerce with the Southwest, encouraged by the fact that steamboats had just started braving the treacherous Missouri River. Becknell's village began cherishing thoughts of competing with St. Louis as America's westernmost window.

Becknell himself immediately planned a far more profitable trip to Sante Fe. In so doing, he introduced to the plains the use of the prairie wagon and the strategy of caravan travel. Both mules and oxen pulled the wagons which were first manufactured near Pittsburgh—Conestogas, which were later replaced by prairie schooners built in western Missouri. During the summer of 1822 Becknell led the first wagon train over a route which thereupon became America's road to Santa Fe and the treasures of the Southwest even though it was a trip requiring great stamina, especially one stretch between the Arkansas and Cimarron rivers infamous for the absence of water. Caravans of considerable size usually followed Becknell's trail because even large groups had good reason to fear the Comanche.

In its day, the Santa Fe trade was enormously important and rewarding. With proper precautions there was no reason to fear that men, beasts, and the wagons filled with shawls, tools, looking glasses, cutlery, and woolens would not cross the plains safely to Santa Fe. Nor would they likely fail to return with silver bullion, mules and mule-breeding stock, furs, and horses for the eastern region. Traders normally could expect 50 percent profit, although 100 percent returns were not uncommon. The advertisements about the commerce with New Mexico soon described goods from New York and Philadelphia which merchants in those distant cities sent to Missouri especially for the caravans which gathered each spring.

A larger result from this triumph on the Santa Fe Trail was the promise that Missouri might become the nation's port for trade with South America. Missouri's Sen. Thomas Hart Benton and others advised cities on the Atlantic Coast that they would actually be closer to Central American trade centers by following the overland route from Missouri. While this vision of Missouri's future never materialized, the notoriety about the tie between Missouri and the provinces of Mexico stimulated national interest in the Southwest so that for the generation growing up in the era of Andrew Jackson, stories of the Santa Fe trail were the means of learning about the nation's vast interior. Many Missourians, however, considered the most remarkable result of the commerce with Mexico to have been the introduction of the mule and silver money throughout the state. Both animal and mineral had a lasting importance in the state's economy, although silver had an immediate blessing. With an ample supply of coins Missouri could cling to cautious economics. Santa Fe silver made it possible for Missouri to condemn the use that most other states were making of paper money.

The Santa Fe Trail continued to attest to Missouri's natural advantage until traffic on the trail was disrupted by the Civil War. Becknell's town of Franklin, however, did not survive to enjoy the prosperity brought by the trail. Once so proud and expectant, Franklin fell victim to the power of the same nature which had briefly promised it such prominence. In 1828, shortly after Kit Carson had left his smithy apprenticeship in Franklin to join the Santa Fe excitement, the implacable Missouri River claimed the town. Franklin simply slid into the water, ending an era as quickly as it had begun. Meanwhile, the steamboats had reached a new favorite, Independence, a town situated on the border near the river. Independence emerged as the seat of Jackson County, created in 1826 after significant migration had reached the state's western boundary. Only St. Louis surpassed Independence in illustrating how nature had given Missouri an extraordinary place in the history of America's growth.

For a quarter-century after 1825, Independence ruled as Queen City of the nation's new empire. Independence was, as Josiah Gregg put it, "the general 'port of embarkation' for every part of the great western and northern 'prairie ocean.' " Gregg's comments were made in his influential book, *Commerce of the Prairies,* first published in 1844. Gregg had a typical early Missouri background as the son of a Kentucky farmer who had moved to Tennessee and Illinois before settling in Missouri in 1812. At age twenty-five, Gregg found his wretched health miraculously improved after making a trip in 1831 along the trail to Santa Fe. By then Independence was the great departing point, and men such as Gregg were in town often. They were not too busy to fail to see that western Missouri was a handsome region. Gregg endorsed a popular description when he told his readers that "the rich and beautiful uplands in the vicinity of Independence might well be denominated the 'garden spot' of the Far West." [4]

4. Josiah Gregg, *Commerce of the Prairies,* 2 vols. (New York: J. and H. G. Langley, 1845), 1: 33, 314.

For Gregg's generation, Independence represented America looking back at the end of one world and peering westward toward another. As time passed, the town dominated the region by launching the nation's march to Oregon and to California while it continued to serve as the emporium for Santa Fe caravans. By the 1840s, traders setting out for the Southwest had to make room around Independence for groups lured by the green of Oregon's lovely pastures and soon by the glitter of California's gold. There must have been awkward moments as Independence played host to traders and trappers starved for whiskey and women as well as to the Presbyterian and Congregational missionaries starting their treks to the Willamette Valley. These spiritual emissaries were followed by a host of settlers who also passed through Independence as they pursued a vision inspired by a Missouri senator.

One of Missouri's and America's most popular United States senators was Lewis Linn, who served in Washington from 1833 until his untimely death ten years later. A physician in Ste. Genevieve who became what many contemporaries called the "model senator," Linn was among the first statesmen to campaign in behalf of the Northwest. His proposals for an Oregon Territory received wide circulation around the United States since Oregon was favorably described at a time when the 1837 depression made many farmers restless for new frontiers. Inspired in large measure by Linn, migrating parties from Missouri, herself often considered an Eden, were heading overland by 1841 for the new paradise in Oregon. When economic conditions improved, Independence was crowded with emigrants who had to prepare for an ordeal of possibly five months. With wagons facing a pull over 2,400 miles of rugged trail, Independence blacksmiths strained to provide needed wagon wheels, chains, axles, linchpins, and spokes. After 1843 the Oregon Trail out of Missouri was as familiar as the Santa Fe route had been twenty years earlier.

Missouri had hardly grown accustomed to the lure of Oregon when gold called men to another region. By April 1849, Independence, along with Westport and St. Joseph, was host to excited prospectors from all over the Union who were bent upon California. Independence was then described as nothing but men, mules, oxen, and wagons. Probably more than 30,000 persons in 1849 followed the Oregon Trail to the point where the path to California began. Even Missourians abandoned their state to join the push: during the gold rush a popular song told of coming all the way from Pike County in old Missouri, and another ballad described "Sweet Betsy of Pike."

Whether from Pike or some other county, Missourians helped fill the new communities in California, Oregon, Washington, New Mexico, and Utah. Furthermore, the type of Missourians who went West was as significant as their numbers: many public officials in the western states bore names familiar in Missouri. Meanwhile, Missouri had become more than a gateway to the great West and mother to many new communities. She also was briefly the center for a thriving overland trade. Mail, stagecoach, and freight all departed from Missouri to cross the plains and mountains. The firm of Russell, Majors, and Waddell was especially important, not only in the Missouri economy, but in strengthening the bridge across Gregg's western ocean. However, the telegraph put an end in 1861 to the year-long career of the firm's Pony Express out of St. Joseph. In doing so, it signaled the distressing changes technology was beginning to impose on Missouri.

The coming of steam power as master to nature brought Missouri only brief triumph before the great tribulation set in. Missouri's finest hour in American history occurred when the United States was an association of regions. Until the Civil War, America was a kind of quilt which nature had patched out of several areas, sewing Missouri into the center. So long as steamboat transportation pilots, overland traders, and trappers were important, questions of distance and commerce were faced in much the same fashion as in the earliest days of civilization. When Missouri was young and dynamic, society still relied on individual ownership and the primacy of family and local culture. Then the railroad appeared, creating new relationships between nature and society. It consolidated America as steamboat, stagecoach, and prairie schooner could not have done, an achievement which greatly diminished the value of Missouri's rich legacy from nature.

For better or worse, America and Missouri began in the 1830s to wrest free from the constraints of nature. The steamboat promised the first new mastery over space since the invention of the wheel. For Missouri and her rivers, the steamboat seemed like a divine reaffirmation, affording travel which left things as they were, requiring no destruction of land and forests and no complicated private or public financial organizations. The short-lived greatness of the steamboat brought another colorful moment for Missouri in American continental development, especially during the 1850s. In that decade St. Louis once more symbolized Missouri's primary place in the flow of American energy by receiving annually more than 3,000 steamboats with nearly a million tons of freight. Small wonder that the great hero of the era was not a military man nor a fur trapper, but a riverboat pilot. Young Sam Clemens shared the vast admiration for these pilots, since in a sense they were the greatest figures in Missouri's history—men who professed to know nothing about machines, but everything about getting the best from nature.

Beginning in 1817, when a primitive steamboat called the *Zebulon Pike* puffed from Louisville to St. Louis in six weeks, the application of steam power to the river challenged courage and patience. Boats on rivers in the Missouri country had to be designed for the hazards of shallow water. On the Missouri River especially, pilots needed what many thought were supernatural talents to move through its ever-changing beds and currents. There were old pilots still living in the 1940s who could recall how the mouth of the Missouri was the place which separated the expert from the ordinary pilot, leaving only skilled pilots to go up "Big Muddy." Whether on the Mississippi or Missouri River, however, there was immeasurable comfort in hearing a crewman proclaim safe water by shouting, "Mark twain!"

By 1830 trips far beyond Independence were routine. In time, good boats with luck could travel in twenty-four hours from St.

Louis to Jefferson City. Vessels leaving New Orleans in 1849 expected to reach St. Louis in three to four days, but ascending the Missouri River was more difficult, and at least a week was required between St. Louis and St. Joseph. Downstream travel cut the time at least by half. For the towns and hamlets along these routes, the steamboat meant a graphic promise of nature's fulfillment. Village newspaper editors, watching boats come and go, wrote of how their part of Missouri was now closely bound to the Atlantic cities, to Europe, and to those Indies which Senator Benton talked about. On the other hand, they also had to describe the terrible steamboat accidents.

A steamboat's life was estimated at five years since sandbars, snags, storms, and ice and logjams took a fierce toll. Within the boat was the frail boiler system that often turned the vessel into a fiery spectacle, which happened in 1852 when 100 Mormons were killed by the explosion of the *Saluda* near Lexington, Missouri. Ten years before, 55 German immigrants had perished near the mouth of the Missouri when the *Edna* erupted. Sixty-seven steamboat accidents were recorded on western waters in 1852, killing 466 persons. These commonplace disasters were often the result of excessive demands for steam power in struggling with the Missouri's relentless current. Such explosions also destroyed glamorous salons, dining areas, and staterooms, accomodations which presented a glimpse of cultivated living not usually seen in the Missouri countryside.

For Missourians, most of whom had settled along rivers as men elsewhere had done for millennia, the alliance between rivers and steam power was reassuring. Steamboats were considered a natural part of a manifestly evident plan for Missouri to stand out in the nation. The appearance of the floating steam engine did not seem to coarsen the beauty of Missouri's Eden, so that men hailed steamboats as supplementing nature, not pillaging it. Owned by individuals or small companies, the steamboat was not seen as a threat to Missouri's concern for simplicity. However, when the 1840s brought federal encouragement for internal improvements, the Missouri legislature resisted using such funds for clearing and improving the rivers. The state appeared reluctant to change the rivers, just as it was loath later to build acceptable highways. For a time this policy seemed justified, for Missouri remained unscathed when other states suffered bankruptcy from the canal craze.

This caution, bred in part by natural advantage, restrained Missouri when the United States turned to the railroad. With the steamboat apparently in a golden age, few Missourians were much stirred by the vision of a continental railroad. They believed that if there was such a route, it must of necessity cross Missouri, confirming St. Louis once again as the hinge between East and West. The state's natural legacy had been so reassuring that those Missourians who thought about a rail link failed to appreciate the consequences of the railroad construction: once it was built, men were no longer obliged to follow natural constraints in traveling across America. Weather, water, and topography had become irrelevant. For optimistic Americans, including many St. Louis citizens, this new development implied that the nineteenth century would be one of human triumph over natural barriers.

Conscious of rail projects to the east, St. Louis leaders tried in the 1830s pushing an indifferent Missouri toward building railroads. From the state came help only of a fumbling and belated character since Missouri at first appeared determined to cling to what she mistakenly considered to be Jacksonian principle by resisting using public funds to build railroads. In 1836–1837, the state chartered eighteen railroad corporations but gave money to none, a record that was momentarily gratifying in the dark days of national depression which followed. Meanwhile, neighboring states such as Illinois, Indiana, Michigan, and Ohio met disaster from financial involvement in canal and rail ventures hastily planned and poorly executed. Further caution came from the claim of many Missourians that, at best, the railroad was merely secondary to the rivers and should be used only where rivers needed connecting.

However, these views and the depression experience were fading by 1849 when a railroad convention met in St. Louis. This gathering, which included many spokesmen for states of the Middle West, was hardly successful from Missouri's standpoint. St. Louis saw its ungrateful convention guests decide to encourage the view that the eastern terminus of a transcontinental rail line ought to be the rising lake town of Chicago. The convention had been unmoved by one of Sen. Thomas Hart Benton's most famous speeches. Once a doubter about railroads himself, Benton now urged a route which would move from San Francisco at one end to St. Louis in the middle and on to the great cities on the Atlantic. In making this appeal, Benton sought to prove that not even a mechanical age would threaten Missouri's central role. He insisted that those who traveled west through Missouri on a transcontinental railroad would know that it was at last the route to the Indies.

Briefly inspired by such reassurance, the Missouri General Assembly incorporated a Pacific Railroad in 1849. This line, along with another struggling rail enterprise, the Hannibal and St. Joseph road, soon received financial help from the once-skeptical state. Then, in the 1850s, Missouri capitulated to a national craze. She aided seven railroads, even permitting the companies to use the credit of Missouri's people. The state issued bonds which were then lent to the railroads, with the public retaining first mortgage while the rail firms sold the bonds. The collaboration became a calamity as costs of construction rose fearfully and more and more aid was requested. Additional bonds were issued and then discounted as buyers hesitated, while building activity faltered and waste increased. By 1861 Missouri had come to believe the railroads had abused the citizens' faith and credit to the amount of nearly $25 million with little to show for it. Only one line was completed when the Civil War broke out—the Hannibal and St. Joseph road, which was 206 miles in length, and cost $58,125 per mile.

The state was now hitched to the machine. After further construction was interrupted by the Civil War, Missouri debated whether there was any choice but to resume her painfully expensive relationship with the railroad. Obviously, more state aid was desperately needed if some tracks were ever to reach useful points, and friends of construction said that despite the earlier fiascoes, postwar recovery and progress depended upon the rails. Consequently, between 1866 and 1872, Missouri's tribute to the locomotive was impressive. So eager were Missouri's

leaders to get a network of railroads running that the general assembly meekly surrendered the public's liens against several
roads. This seemed the only means, short of unthinkable public
ownership, to get construction finished. The gesture left the
people rather than the rail companies with debts of virtually $25
million, as well as doubts about honesty in the state capital.
Rumors of legislative bribery, or "boodle" as it was then
called, persisted throughout the ordeal. Once they assumed the
terrible costs which the railroads had skillfully eluded, the
people of Missouri struggled until 1903 with the debts cheerfully
incurred by their legislators. Both the state constitutions of 1865
and of 1875 forbade further state loans to railroads, a mark of
the rebirth of Missouri conservatism.

In an age known for its corruption at both state and national
levels, a much-shaken Missouri did see some rail lines completed. The Pacific road reached Kansas City in 1865, but not
before $6 million belonging to the taxpayers was given away
when the company was excused from its debts. By 1870, the
Atlantic and Pacific Company arrived in jubilant Springfield
while the Iron Mountain line had descended from St. Louis into
the bootheel area by 1872. North of the Missouri River, tracks
extended from St. Louis through Macon and Kirksville to the
Iowa border by 1868. However, the machine proved a very
mixed blessing. Citizens who had been led to expect reasonable
freight rates instead faced discrimination behind the fixing of
charges. This injustice angered communities and counties, many
of whom had mortgaged themselves to secure these lines or
their branches. Some localities repudiated their indebtedness,
often incurred in county bonds which railroad promoters had instigated, and this disavowal of debt brought about a long furor.
The last of local debts from the railroad extravaganza was not
retired until 1940.

In many ways the machine proved much harder to live with
than the river, besides being more controversial. Although Missouri finally achieved a modest rail system, for which she had
paid heavily while watching ownership go to corporations remote from the state, the experience served to deepen citizen suspicions about using public money for general improvement

schemes. The debts and the skepticism left by the railroad disgrace haunted later generations in Missouri, making it especially
difficult for those who urged that the public should support
highways, education, and various humane projects. Finally,
men who had dreamed of national eminence for Missouri
through machine power were profoundly disappointed. Despite
her expensive attempts, Missouri no longer could claim after
1875 the powerful physical place in the Union which had been
hers in the 1830s.

The trail caravan, the steamboat, the pony express rider, all
became obsolete in the wake of progress. Even Independence
suffered. The Queen City's problems began when steam travel
on the river became more significant. Since Independence was a
few miles distant from the Missouri, Kansas City's location on
the river's bank gave it a dramatic advantage. By 1860, the up-
start Kansas City had a population of 4,418 while Independence
had become a quiet dowager with a population sagging to
3,164. However, Kansas City faced the grim fact that the continent's transportation center had become Chicago; even the Hannibal and St. Joseph Railroad across northern Missouri linked
with Chicago rather than St. Louis. Consequently, Kansas City
was obliged to become a fief of Chicago by building a bridge in
1869 across the once-dominant Missouri River in order to con-
nect the city with the Hannibal and St. Joe line and thus with
the new national transportation pattern. When this tie was made,
the great West and the nation no longer needed to acknowledge
the presence and power of St. Louis, the Missouri River, and
Independence. Kansas City's submission showed how Missouri
had to settle for an increasingly modest role in America's development while other states assumed more dominant positions.

There had, however, been one last effort at keeping Missouri's natural eminence. This try required the sort of courage
and gallantry which were admired in Boone's and Becknell's
time, especially since the Mississippi River provided the setting
for this episode. One of Chicago's great advantages was its
early connection with two railroad bridges spanning the upper
Mississippi. Most Missourians glumly supposed that the mighty
torrent sweeping past St. Louis could never be bridged. Yet if

that desperate city were to compete with Chicago for continental supremacy, a bridge must somehow link it with the eastern railroads. To wide amazement such a span was built by James Buchanan Eads. Becoming a Missourian at age thirteen, Eads never lost his regard for the rivers in his region. He had worked on a steamboat, something he, like Sam Clemens, never forgot, so that eventually Eads became famous for solving difficulties long associated with rivers. His design of ironclad boats helped produce a Federal victory on the Mississippi during the Civil War, and Eads conceived a method for using jetties at the Mississippi's mouth that allowed the river itself to remove sediment from its bed, thus opening the port of New Orleans to large ships after 1879. Techniques originated by Eads for salvaging materials on river bottoms were spectacularly successful but he did not live to pursue plans for an isthmian canal.

For his cherished city of St. Louis Eads achieved his supreme triumph. He completed one of the world's great bridges in 1874, a feat made possible by a miracle of masonry foundations that dropped nearly 130 feet below the river to the stone bed. The first bridge whose superstructure was fashioned from steel, it was a cantilever design with two levels, one for railroads and the other for vehicles. Ead's bridge was an achievement for which many persons sought to share credit, including Andrew Carnegie, but only after Eads himself had guided the project through enormous political, economic, and technical difficulties. On 4 July 1874, Missouri was host to one of the great public occasions for which that florid age was famous when the Eads bridge, instantly a world wonder, was dedicated. President U. S. Grant and a host of politicians and financiers attended to offer tribute.

At the ceremonies were many citizens who hoped the homage was actually being paid to the restoration of St. Louis as the nation's most influential and useful city. This hope was not to be fulfilled. In spite of the genius and heroism of Eads, the bunting-draped engines parading across the new marvel, and the cheering crowds, Missouri's natural legacy was no longer sufficient for continental greatness. Chicago, with its great rail connections, nearby iron ore, coal fields, and steel mills, now led. Out of this struggle, however, a Missourian had won lasting distinction. In 1884, James B. Eads was the first foreigner to receive the Albert Medal from Queen Victoria. Impressive honors continued into the twentieth century, long after Eads's death. He was selected by a group of experts as one of history's five greatest engineers and, in 1920, he, Samuel Clemens, and Daniel Boone were the three Missourians elected to the Hall of Fame for Great Americans at New York University. In 1929 New Orleans held a golden jubilee honoring Eads's memory.

A hundred years after Eads finished his masterpiece, Missouri and her sister states were trying to confront a crisis over nature's legacy. Such treasures as clean air, fresh streams, massive forests, generous mineral deposits, and fertile soil had either been squandered or abused. The profligacy of past generations added a touch of pathos in 1976 to the glittering steel arch which arose along the Mississippi next to the Eads bridge. The memorial to Jefferson's continental dream attested to more than the great western kingdom extending across Missouri and beyond. It brought to mind also the hopeful newcomers who once had hastened into Missouri to share a land famed for variety and abundance. Yet while many Missourians came to cherish nature's legacy, they were joined by others who managed before the nation was two hundred years old to despoil much of the state's natural bequest which men in Jefferson's time believed would last forever.

4

More Than One Missouri

$\mathcal{M}$ ISSOURI's character combines several strains derived from the variety of her physical settings and types of citizens. Observers of the state have usually pointed to four or more segments which were set off by physical uniqueness and social viewpoint. Those were the Ozark highlands or mountain country; the region known as Little Dixie; and the two cities St. Louis and Kansas City, which stood at opposite edges of the state. While these four parts perhaps offered the most striking differences, there were at least two more Missouris which stood in contrast. One was the bootheel region in the southeastern quarter of the state, where a bit of the Mississippi's rich, flat plain was located. The other was the prairie area embracing many of the western counties and reaching into the state north of the Missouri River. Out of this tangle of locales developed Missouri's major traditions and important experiences.

So varied has Missouri been that even the pronunciation of the state's name remains a cause of disagreement. As was true in so many matters, the division lay often between country folk and city people, as well as between one geographic section and another. Generally, citizens of longest standing and deepest regard for the state's spirit have said "Muh-zoo-rah." The less knowledgeable residents have settled for the simpler, newer "Muh-zoo-ree." Not only was there more than one Missouri in form and word, but these various parts of the state traditionally

72

warred among themselves in spirit. The two cities had a scorn for each other matched only by their disdain for the countryside lying between them. This antipathy helped assure that viewpoints in Little Dixie, the Ozark Hills, the bootheel, and the plains would dominate in Missouri. The prevailing outlook from the farms and small towns revealed the resentment the outstate area felt toward the two cities. Both Kansas City and St. Louis habitually professed preferences for interests and ideas outside Missouri. Consequently, while the two cities came in time to possess the majority of Missourians by count, they remained divided and therefore helpless before the persisting outlook in Little Dixie, the Ozarks, the plains country, and the bootheel. In those parts of Missouri, people were bound by the Jeffersonian suspicion of cities. It was reflected especially in the power these areas retained in the general assembly.

Traditions which Americans would be most likely to associate with Missouri flourished in Little Dixie and the Ozark Hills, although the two areas were themselves superficial foes politically—the former Democratic and the latter Republican. The Ozark area was an entrancing region of mountains and hollows, bluffs and caves, and rivers and springs. The people took such delight in their part of Missouri that they usually opposed any venture or idea alien to their ways. The proud native reply to the suggestion that the Ozark Mountains were not really very high was that the hollows between the hills were very deep. Over generations, the Ozark Missourians stubbornly persisted as their region courted what outsiders considered economic and social disaster.

Embracing as it did much of the state south of the Missouri River, the Ozark highlands prospered in little but beauty and in the lure of wildlife. Even these attributes were threatened by decades of exploitation which saw the Ozark forests cut away, the devastating invasion and subsequent retreat of mining en-
·terprise, and the erosion of the thin soil by agricultural struggles on hillsides ill-suited to farming. More recently, forest preservation, the enactment of the Ozark National Scenic Riverways Act in 1964, the adoption of better agricultural and reforestation techniques, and the expansion of poultry and cattle production,

all brought the Ozark Missourians out of one predicament. They had thereupon to face a new difficulty. In the last part of the twentieth century the Ozarks were threatened again, this time by tourism and herbicides which promised a renewed menace to this unique part of Missouri and America.

There was no question about the rising appeal of Missouri's Ozark countryside. Evidence of this was ample in Congress's decision in 1964 to keep unspoiled some 52,000 acres along 134 miles of the spectacularly beautiful Current River. Elsewhere, this land of swift streams was being altered into a chain of man-made lakes. As early as the 1930s, the creation of the Lake of the Ozarks brought noise, lights, and shabbiness to the winding roads and to the small communities surrounding the lake. It was not long before those who came to find quiet and beauty in the hills around Branson encountered snail-paced traffic lines heading for widely advertised entertainment spots like "Silver Dollar City." Tourism and the Ozarks were often poorly yoked.

Nevertheless, for more than a century much of the Ozark highlands managed, as bits of the region still do, to resist the new approaches to life. Here persisted many customs and some of the language from Europe which came to the area before the Civil War. These Ozark Missourians, frequently Scotch-Irish, Welsh, or English in descent, early found that the best manner of living in their region, whether it was along Cane Creek or near Eminence, was not to violate the wilderness but to dwell peaceably with it. As a result of this uncharacteristic rejection of the American zest to remake the countryside, many of Missouri's citizens thus entered the atomic age on small clearings, content with modest pastures.

In this fashion the Missouri of the Ozarks lingered as a hilly country of proud, conservative, deeply religious, and usually poor people. Though agricultural extension service and national forest management did promise to strengthen the economic endeavor of the region, many sections of the Ozarks retained the outlook of 1876 in 1976. For these Missourians there was no controversy over the supremacy of the male, the importance of the camp meeting and religious enthusiasm, or the vitality of the complete family which embraced all persons among the hills reasonably related by birth or marriage. In a sense, this part of Missouri turned simplicity into a sophisticated art. Although the interest and enthusiasm of tourists, sociologists, and folklorists may have redoubled the canniness of some Ozark citizens, nevertheless these Missourians remained at heart devoted to the old Jacobite ballads, the "shivaree" fun after weddings, and the clear understanding that most drudgery was women's work.

In moving from the Ozark Mountains north by highway 63 through Howell, Texas, and Phelps counties and thence passing across bits of Maries, Osage, and Cole counties, the traveler reaches the Missouri River at Jefferson City. Immediately after saluting Thomas Jefferson's statue before the capitol and crossing the bridge, the observer enters Callaway and quickly thereafter Boone County, two pillars of Little Dixie. By Missouri standards this influential region is ancient, growing from settlements which sprang up after 1810. Newcomers, mostly southern slaveholders, rejected the surroundings of St. Charles and St. Louis to go to the middle of the state, drawn by the appeal of the area around Boone's Lick—more popularly Boonslick. The Boone family and others had opened the countryside of what became Howard, Boone, and Callaway counties.

A great rush of settlement in the 1820s responded to stories of the area's fine deep loess soil, its gently rolling terrain, its abundance of salt and timber, all of which could be found so near the mighty river as it coursed through the middle of the state. In such handsome surroundings a manner of living was sought by many early Missourians that could only be called aristocratically southern. Such an outlook was nurtured for much more than a century in these river valley counties, and soon reached into Audrain, Monroe, and Randolph counties. Since slave-based society appeared to prosper in this part of Missouri, other communities claimed admission to Little Dixie. Even a century after the Civil War, counties such as Shelby, Macon, Chariton, and Saline, as well as Lewis, Pike, Ralls, Lincoln, and Marion along the upper Mississippi, were still considered comrades within this fraternity.

In 1860, Little Dixie included areas which had as many as one slave for every white citizen. The bulk of the state's slave population was there, although any resemblance of the area's society and economy to that of the southern plantation states was far more imagined than real. However, after the Civil War, Little Dixie citizens redoubled efforts to foster what were re-membered as some of the qualities of southern life. This meant an emphasis on discriminating between blacks and whites, on upholding the most conservative arm of the Democratic party, and on encouraging styles in architecture, cooking, sport, and recreation presumed to be part of the southern tradition.

In time, some citizens in the Little Dixie counties found the southern affectation only amusing or disgusting. Yet for a sig-nificant and influential part of the population, preserving a landed aristocratic view was consoling and necessary. Many of the Little Dixie counties once were among the state's wealthiest and most dynamic units. Thanks to the river link, they were in touch with the beloved culture of the South itself, far down-stream. When the railroad seized the North American continent, location along a great river suddenly counted for less. Even so, Little Dixie was either indifferent or opposed to the railway's advent, and the iron machine in return did little for the region. As a result, after 1870 towns and counties in central Missouri lost their prominence. Little Dixie was left to take consolation in preservation of the past and artful use of power in the Mis-souri General Assembly.

With the impact of World War II, air travel, superhighways, and education, Little Dixie surrendered to new economic oppor-tunities and occasionally even to new ideas. Integration on the University of Missouri's campus, located in Little Dixie's Boone County, tended to diminish the venerable class and racial distinctions cherished by some local citizens. Also after 1945, scholarship at the university began to compete with the zest for bourbon whiskey and major athletics which earlier had brought the institution fame of a sort. This repute had been considered appropriate by youths who came to Little Dixie seeking the badges of male attainment said to be recognized on campuses and in society down the Mississippi River.

Even with these changes, life for Missourians in Little Dixie

as on the Ozark mountainside, in the bootheel, or out on the
prairie remained markedly different from that in the business offices of St. Louis and in the Country Club district of Kansas
City. Each town had its own extraordinary character, adding
much to the variety of Missouri. For most of the nineteenth century St. Louis rejoiced in great expectations and no small
achievements. Dreams of national eminence arose from a splendid geographic location and from cultural distinction, so that by
the time the United States celebrated its 1876 centennial, St.
Louis citizens spoke earnestly of replacing Washington as the
federal capital. However, this national movement to the bank of
the Mississippi was foreseen as a tribute to St. Louis and not to
the state, which the city saw as a sort of backcountry beyond the
city. From the early days of statehood, St. Louis and Missouri
had exchanged suspicion and mistrust, in part because St. Louis
had never been a simple frontier village, which outstate Missouri found disconcerting. St. Louis's beginnings had left a culture which was strange indeed to the Missourians struggling on
the banks of the Osage or the Grand in their rude huts.

These yeomen who made up the bulk of Missouri's population evidently held a mixed attitude of awe and hate as they
watched the progress of St. Louis which, by 1850, was remarkable for growth and diversity. From an 1837 population of
20,000, St. Louis moved to 75,000 in 1850 and 160,000 in
1860. Before this rate of increase began to slow in 1880, St.
Louis boasted of 350,000 residents. There had been dividends
in the years when Missouri and surrounding regions had depended upon St. Louis in commercial, fiscal, and professional
matters. Probably no one in the town was surprised when Ralph
Waldo Emerson in 1852 solemnly predicted a splendid future
for St. Louis. Emerson was one of many emissaries from the
realm of letters and arts who were nearly overwhelmed by nineteenth-century St. Louis. Less impressed were the farmers and
village residents across the state. However, their spokesmen had
to struggle not to be intimidated in the general assembly by the
representatives of the great city. In turn, the urban delegation to
Jefferson City considered the state's outlook unimaginative and

paralyzing. The quarrel between St. Louis and much of outlying Missouri over railroads and banking displayed the awkwardness of ill-matched interests and beliefs.

By 1850 it seemed nothing could hinder St. Louis's march toward the anticipated millions in population and an influence from the Atlantic to the Pacific, as well as from the Great Lakes to the Gulf. At mid-century the city had recently withstood blows which might have crushed lesser towns. Rural Missourians seeing St. Louis as a tower of evil could have considered two ghastly events of 1849 as richly deserved retribution. First was the burning of St. Louis's famed waterfront, six miles in length, where 170 boats at a time could press for places. On 17 May 1849, the steamboat *White Cloud* went ablaze, beginning a conflagration in which fifteen business blocks were consumed at a cost to St. Louis estimated at $6 million.

While the city struggled with this disaster, a savage invasion of Asiatic cholera began. This disease, one of the era's great killers, had visited St. Louis before, and would appear again. In 1849, however, the plague was the worst in the state's history, aggravating the rural skepticism toward the city since St. Louis was blamed for the disease spreading across Missouri's countryside. The city itself was cruelly hit, with nearly 2,000 persons lost to the illness in June alone. After 5,000 deaths, St. Louis created a powerful committee of safety which impressively directed efforts to control the epidemic and to clean up after the fire. A quarter-century later, the city learned that its wretched water and sewer systems made an ideal breeding place for the newly discovered bacterial cause of cholera.

For a time not even these cataclysms of flame and death seemed to thwart St. Louis's move toward greatness. It emerged rebuilt and improved, proud of such adornments as the Planter's House, reputedly the finest hotel in all the West. Here in the 1850s came guests from throughout the world—English noblemen, eastern speculators, steamboat captains, Indian chiefs, southern agriculturists—to gather in the hotel's splendid bar where the highball was created. This saloon was called the nerve center of two great river valleys, and its guests toasted the city's limitless future with Planter's Punch, a potion invented by the house. The hotel's name was a bit misleading, however, since by 1850 St. Louis was renowned as an industrial and commercial leader, not a patrician, agricultural center. Iron goods, flour, fabrics, foodstuffs, and distilled commodities were all produced and distributed by the city in impressive amounts. The Civil War only enhanced St. Louis's economic prowess, for the value of manufacturing there increased by virtually 300 percent.

Amid this material achievement, St. Louis enjoyed numerous cultural amenities: the nation's second-oldest symphony orchestra, an opera (sung in St. Louis long before Chicago even existed), and a professional theater that had flourished since 1835. Downtown at the Mercantile Library, the city's elite heard lecturers such as Emerson, Bronson Alcott, Charles Dickens, and William M. Thackeray. The library held the city's first public exhibition of art while it was assembling one of the nation's finest collections of books and periodicals. Another kind of cultural enrichment came with the thirty-six breweries which flourished in St. Louis by 1854 as well as with the German immigrants who believed Sundays should not be limited to piety.

The tension between this sprightly city and the rest of nineteenth-century Missouri was exemplified in the strain dividing St. Louis from surrounding St. Louis County. From the start, the city had been restless in this enforced companionship, and the rural environs seemed to lack respect for their city "betters." The latter believed that it was county influence which made the general assembly often change St. Louis's charter. The county's use of its tax power in what the city considered an unfair way was a regular cause of rage. Finally, after a half-century of acrimony, a new state constitution permitted St. Louis in 1876 to move about as far toward independence as possible while yet remaining part of Missouri.

With home rule and separation from the county attained, St. Louis thought it had put aside the last restraints for greatness. The city had disregarded suggestions that it consolidate with the county. Instead, the constitutional convention of 1875 was reminded by tactless city representatives like Joseph Pulitzer that St. Louis was a small state of its own. Replies from outstate delegates sought to shame the city by pointing out that it never had tried to become an integral part of Missouri. Nevertheless, a year later St. Louis became autonomous, escaping the county with forty-three additional square miles which were believed adequate for all future growth. Most gratifying to the city, however, was the sense of emancipation from the uncomprehending and debilitating rural outlook in the county and in Jefferson City.

Soon the city found it had won a Pyrrhic victory. As talk of becoming the new national capital dwindled, observers across Missouri watched St. Louis topple to the classic evils that country folk eagerly associated with cities. St. Louis's growth began a significant slowing. Its reputation became more one of unkemptness and smokiness than beauty. Its once-proud elitist leadership seemed to wither into cautious or indifferent conservatism. When corruption and slovenliness overcame the city in the 1890s, members of the St. Louis aristocracy exhibited a near-criminal obliviousness. By then, even the cherished Mississippi River had earned a reputation for filthiness.

In time, the county of St. Louis surpassed the old, constricted city in population and wealth. The once fabled town was left on the river's bank, nominally free, but increasingly forlorn. Between 1876 and 1976, St. Louis slowly discovered that a splendid isolation and a preoccupation with the concerns of the Atlantic seaboard and Europe ultimately could not erase the fact that it was part of Missouri. Even so, the news seemed not to alter the city's ancient disdain for most things Missourian. The cleavage between city and state remained deep and divisive through three-quarters of the twentieth century. Rural Missourians saw in the fate of St. Louis an appropriate confirmation of the old agrarian misgiving about urban life.

Whereas St. Louis existed long before statehood, Missouri's second great city did not develop until after the Civil War. Actually, Kansas City began pushing forward as a metropolis of national consequence just when St. Louis saw her anticipated glory fade. While Kansas City remained very different from St. Louis in composition and outlook, there was one similarity, for in its own way, Kansas City grew up estranged from the state. Once again Missouri had failed to establish any significant comradeship with a major city within her borders. This left Missouri squeezed between two powerful communities whose physical locations were barely within the state and whose perspectives looked beyond rather than into Missouri. Furthermore, though they were separated by less than 300 miles, two more different communities than St. Louis and Kansas City would have been difficult to devise. The two cities gave thanks that, whatever else might go wrong, each was wholly unlike the other.

Two influences especially affected Kansas City's participation in the history of Missouri and America. One of these was a matter of setting; the other involved an enduring point of view. Kansas City's location was striking, being just where the Missouri River abruptly changed its southern descent to an easterly course across the state. This elbow marked the first point at which streams and overland travel eastward from the plains could reach the river and rail connections with the older markets. Just as St. Louis had kept its interests and values toward the East, Kansas City's concern from the start was for the products and people of the western plains. This origin was profoundly important because of the independent posture it tempted each city to take, for the strength of neither community was derived from the state which claimed it. On one occasion, citizens of Kansas City responded delightedly to a proposal for annexation from the state of Kansas. Only Missouri's legislative refusal to separate kept Kansas City from joining a state whose western spirit seemed more congenial.

The second shaping influence on Kansas City was that it began and remained as a speculative venture—the city was established by a private company. Near-fatal conditions between 1855 and 1865 encouraged a Kansas City obsession with success which showed itself especially in boasts about its material prospects. From the 1870s through the 1970s, Kansas City remained preoccupied with the future, its stress on the "about to be" remaining so markedly materialist that the town could never successfully claim intellectual or cultural achievements comparable to those of St. Louis. Kansas City never quite forgot that it was a struggling river hamlet in the 1850s with only a better position for river commerce to distinguish it from Independence.

While Kansas City insisted on 1850 as its founding year, deterrents of cholera and border warfare kept the village a frail beginning until after 1865. Throughout that interlude, the small group of men who had founded Kansas City as a speculation stubbornly insisted that their investment had a future. It was the determination of these men who glimpsed a golden lining in the black clouds over Kansas City after 1855 which somehow sustained the frontier hamlet through border ruffianism and civil conflict. One of these men, Robert Van Horn, especially embodied the tendency which kept Kansas City pointed toward maturity.

Born in Pennsylvania, Van Horn was thirty years old when he reached Kansas City in 1854 to become nominally a journalist but largely a goad for development, a role he continued until his death in 1916. Van Horn's career was, to say the least, energetic. He led a Union battalion in the Civil War, and then served Kansas City as mayor, state senator, and congressman on three separate occasions. In these activities Van Horn kept insisting that something important eventually would happen to Kansas City. It was he who brought telegraph lines into Kansas City at an early point, probably saving his town from drowning in the wake of the then-fast-moving city of St. Joseph located just up the river. Van Horn and his colleagues took seriously the writings of author William Gilpin who lived in nearby Independence. Gilpin stressed the future worldwide importance for the middle of America. Van Horn evidently sensed what geographers and economists were later to point out—that a vast area southwest, west, and northwest of Kansas City drained to that city's very feet. From this dim perspective, Van Horn helped establish Kansas City's almost religious faith in her natural triumph as the dominant metropolis of the continent. Van Horn's vision was sustained by the practical realization that railroad links must tie Kansas City with Chicago.

After the 1870s, Kansas City's posture was as inclined toward time ahead as St. Louis's outlook came to revere time past. For one thing, Kansas City's growth suddenly became ex-

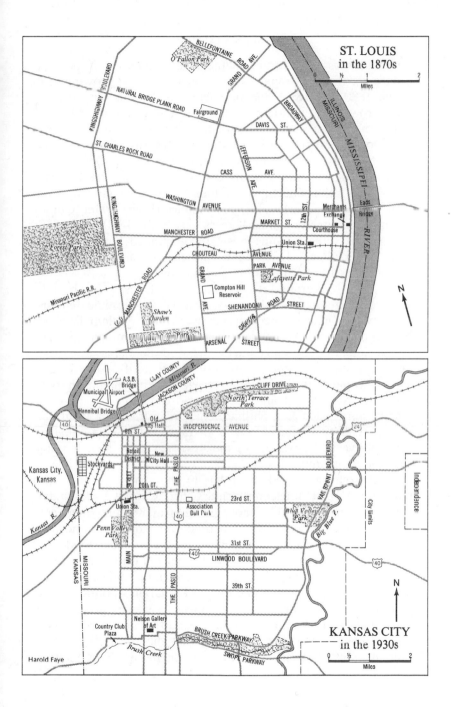

ST. LOUIS
in the 1870s

0   ½   1   2
Miles

BELLEFONTAINE ROAD AVE.
O'Fallon Park
GRAND
FLORISSANT BOULEVARD
NATURAL BRIDGE PLANK ROAD
BROADWAY
Fairground
DAVIS ST.
KINGSHIGHWAY
ST. CHARLES ROCK ROAD
JEFFERSON
CASS   AVE.
WASHINGTON   AVENUE
12th ST.
Merchants Exchange
Eads Bridge
KING HIGHWAY BOULEVARD
MARKET ST.
Courthouse
MANCHESTER   ROAD
Union Sta.
Forest Park
CHOUTEAU   AVENUE
MANCHESTER ROAD
PARK   AVENUE
GRAND   AVE.
Compton Hill Reservoir
Lafayette Park
Missouri Pacific R.R.
SHENANDOAH   ROAD   STREET
OSAGE
Shaw's Garden
ILLINOIS
MISSOURI
MISSISSIPPI RIVER
N

ARSENAL   STREET

Harold Faye

A.S.B. Bridge
Municipal Airport
Hannibal Bridge
CLAY COUNTY
Missouri R.
JACKSON COUNTY
CLIFF DRIVE
North Terrace Park
40
Old City Hall
6th ST.
INDEPENDENCE   AVENUE
24
Retail District
New City Hall
THE PASEO
VAN BRUNT BOULEVARD
Independence
Kansas City, Kansas
Stockyards
COAL GT.
23rd ST.
Association Ball Park
40
Blue Valley Park
City Limits
Union Sta.
Big Blue R.
Penn Valley Park
MISSOURI
KANSAS
MAIN
31st ST.
LINWOOD BOULEVARD
40
40
Kansas R.
THE PASEO
39th ST.
N
Nelson Gallery of Art
Country Club Plaza
BRUSH CREEK PARKWAY
KANSAS CITY
in the 1930s
Brush Creek
SWOPE PARKWAY
0   ½   1   2
Miles

traordinary, as when in the 1870s alone it increased 70 percent, a pace six times as rapid as St. Louis was then growing. Between 1880 and 1890, the population of Kansas City tripled. Such growth was important since such figures attracted the enthusiasm and the money of investors from the East. Strangely, much of the crucial early support for Kansas City's survival came from Boston speculators, with even the descendants of John and John Quincy Adams putting money into land, stockyards, and rail connections. Joining many other citizens from New England, Charles Francis Adams II and John Quincy Adams II frequently visited Kansas City in the 1880s and 1890s looking for some genuine basis for continued hope amid the mud, the ravines, the blatant hucksterism, and the bravado which seemed to be the essence of the town.

With this background it was natural that Kansas City became a place where individualism was carried to supreme lengths. The town's one genuine cultural jewel, the William Rockhill Nelson Gallery of Art, was an individual's dream and gift. The famed Country Club Plaza business and residential area, with its derivative character mixing southwestern motifs with Spanish style, was the result of speculative wizardry by another individual, J. C. Nichols. Meanwhile, enterprises calling upon a community spirit, such as a philharmonic orchestra and a local university, either faltered or lived in rags. While individualism could thrive in Kansas City, the town never attained a stable spirit of community.

If Missouri appeared an Eden to the many persons who reached her in the nineteenth century, hers was not a simple garden. Newcomers quickly discovered the sharp topographical, economic, and social contrasts that produced more than one Missouri. The state's history, therefore, cannot be understood apart from the fact that her citizens lived in widely differing settings, whether river valleys, city streets, or mountainsides. This fact has led some analysts to argue that a Missourian's political viewpoint derived from his location. Others, however, prefer to recall the legacy that came from the great differences among those who settled in Missouri, insisting that the diversity of Missouri manifested itself as much in its people as its geography.

5

The Many Missourians

NTO Missouri's several settings came a diversity of people. Missouri represented the vanguard of America's frontier, building her culture therefore from the contribution of red, black, and white men and women. Out of New England, the Middle Atlantic region, the Ohio valley, the South, and Europe arrived such an assortment of settlers as would never melt into a bland mixture. The flood tide of this mighty migration into Missouri coincided with the time when the state was most prominent in national affairs. In 1810 the territory's population was around 20,000. Expansion by 1820 brought that figure to nearly 67,000 of whom more than 10,000 were slaves. This number at least doubled in the next decade, and in 1850 there were nearly 700,000 inhabitants. By 1860 Missouri's population passed the million mark, an achievement which put the state eighth in size among members of the Union. She had been twenty-third in 1820.

Then Missouri's growth rate slowed appreciably. In 1870 the population numbered 1,721,295; in 1880 it was 2,168,380; and in 1890, 2,679,183. The rate continued to falter, and in 1930 the total was only 3,629,367, obliging the state to surrender three congressional seats to more dynamic states. Two more members of Congress were stripped away in 1950, and yet another in 1960 as the state grew at the rate of barely 9 percent while the national pace was more than twice that. Ranked fifth in 1900, Missouri fell to thirteenth in 1960. The 1970 census figure of 4,677,399 maintained this pattern.

Ironically, the story of Missouri's growth actually started with an effort to reduce the population. When Americans began arriving in Missouri they showed a distinct hostility to the area's earliest inhabitants, the Indians and the French. By 1821 these groups were receding into legend, some absorbed by the "American" outlook, others abliged to retreat before it. The presence of the Old World cultures, the French and the less significant Spanish, dwindled to place names faintly reminiscent of departed customs. From the Americans came such an impetuous interest in putting Missouri under cultivation that the comparatively relaxed and graceful ways of the French were soon obliterated, except among some families in St. Louis, Ste. Genevieve, and the lead mining areas. Few Americans had time to enjoy the niceties of cooking, clothing, and etiquette which once were nurtured in the French hamlets. The French and Spanish soon passed into the realm of folklore and antiquarian preservation, taking with them an unusual capacity for peaceful existence.

The fate of the very first Missourians was less tranquil. These were the local Indians and those from east of the Mississippi who were being pushed west by the Anglo-American tide. For a time Missouri was the center of U.S. efforts to resolve permanently the problem of coexistence between red and white peoples. Such a policy was based on negotiation and solemn agreement establishing the sanctity of future tribal location. This pact was consummated when the Indians consented to move beyond what was considered the reach of white settlement, which meant to havens west of the Mississippi. Consequently, even after statehood Missouri had a variety of resident and transient Indian tribes within her borders. In 1820 there were still approximately 6,000 Indians scattered across Missouri, whose white citizens grumbled that federal patience and kindness were being lavished upon marauders who received lovely parts of the state as kingdoms.

The original Missouri tribe had been so weakened by disease and intertribal war that it disintegrated before 1800. Thereafter, the federal government sought a permanent dwelling within Missouri for such groups as the Osage, Sac, Fox, Shawnee, and Delaware. There were no more impressive American Indians than the Osage. They had been in Missouri early, living near the mouth of the Osage River when the region was first explored. With a splendid physical presence to bolster their lofty intelligence, the Osage displayed considerable insight about the greed of the paleskins. The white men usually saw all Indians, including the Osage, as hopeless degenerates upon whom it would be sinful to waste an acre of Missouri's marvelous land. Disdaining to adopt the white man's crassness, the Osage leadership was nevertheless powerless to combat white "civilization." With the encroachment of whites came disease, violence, and illicit traffic in whiskey, to say nothing of broken pledges.

After reaching statehood, Missouri became less disposed to be patient or sympathetic with the confused and embattled red man. Even before formally entering the Union, the general assembly asked Congress early in 1821 to halt all Indian immigration into Missouri, to remove all tribes recently pushed into the state from the East, and to nullify all claims to land by the Indians. So determined was Missouri to keep her precious countryside from being wasted on the Indian that there was no hope the Indian presence would somehow survive.

The federal government yielded to white Missouri, despite the fact that there had been an encouraging lack of violence between Indians and whites in the area. Officials in Washington did as Missouri insisted, devoting the 1820s to breaking sacred pledges made to the tribes when they reluctantly had moved across the Mississippi. It meant prying tribes out of the Missouri land assigned to them. In 1825, the Osage surrendered their holdings, which closed a notable effort at Fort Osage, located on the Missouri River near Independence, to accommodate the mutual interests of both white and red residents. This post had been established as a center for peaceable trading and growing understanding in 1808 when the area surrounding Fort Osage appeared well beyond the pressure of white settlement. No one foresaw the speed with which a white tide would roll up the Missouri River valley. Along with the Osage removal went the

Sac, Fox, and Iowa tribes. Soon the Shawnees were ousted from southeastern Missouri, the Delaware from the southwest, and the Kansas group from the western border. Missouri officials tried to hasten the evacuation by authorizing any posse to deal harshly with braves who lingered through stubbornness or forgetfulness.

Despite the alacrity with which the federal government broke its word with several tribes in response to Missouri's clamor, the new state remained unsatisifed. The white man's determination to have all valuable land for himself made Missouri covet two million choice acres just beyond her northwestern border. The first western boundary of the state was a north-south line drawn through the juncture of the Kansas and Missouri rivers and which therefore excluded from Missouri the rich bottom lands along the Platte, Nodaway, and Missouri rivers. It was an area the federal government considered ideal for assignment to Indians being pushed westward. As early as 1830 Missouri began protesting what she alleged was the squandering of such magnificent land. Washington, meanwhile, continued awarding Indians title to what had come to be known as the Platte region, with solemn guarantees of undisturbed possession as well as protection against all other claimants. Undaunted, Missouri's general assembly along with Senators Benton and Linn tried every stratagem to oust all Indians from the Platte country and to move the state boundary westward to the mid-stream of the Missouri River, thereby embracing the coveted Platte land.

For a time, however, President Andrew Jackson appeared to want the Platte area saved for the red man while Congress seemed willing enough to banish the Indians but was loath to enlarge Missouri's boundary. Missouri, however, wanted everything. Eventually Jackson's reluctance to see the federal government again violate its word to the Indians was overcome. By 1836 the clamor of white Missourians was successful and the 1830 Treaty of Prairie du Chien was abrogated, an agreement in which the United States had pledged with several tribes that the Platte region would forever be occupied by the Indians. The Sioux gave up for $400 in gifts, and the Iowa, Sac, and Fox rights cost the United States $7,500 and new guarantees of homes farther west. Several other tribes departed with goods amounting to $4,520, so that late in 1836, the rich soil of the Platte area had been retrieved from the Indian. Upon taking of fice in 1837, President Martin Van Buren officially affirmed Congress's decision that Missouri's boundary was shoved west to the Missouri River. This achievement for white superiority and state prestige caused wide rejoicing in the state, and after bonfires, speeches, and refreshments to celebrate the new acquisition, many Missourians hastened into the promised land. Soon nearly 4,500 whites with their black slaves had entered the Platte country with the civilization which many red chiefs had denounced as ignoble.

Thanks to the reluctant co-operation of Congress and Presidents Jackson and Van Buren, Missouri's population was reduced to black and white only—no red. Racial and ethnic diversity continued, however, as Missouri rapidly acquired a mixture of peoples and cultures. Newcomers hastened from the South, the northeastern states, and from principalities in Germany. So many immigrants from Kentucky and Tennessee had taken possession of Missouri that there were jokes about those two older states disappearing. Most of these settlers joined others who had been eager to till the land, so that by 1820 more than three-quarters of Missourians were farmers. The rising rural population soon threatened the old political establishment in St. Louis. For a time the preponderance of newcomers continued to arrive from Kentucky, Tennessee, North Carolina, and Virginia, bringing with them appetizing traditions for curing hams, frying chickens, and distilling corn whiskey, as well as importing some arresting ideas about individualism.

Most of the southerners emigrating to Missouri were unaccustomed to life on large plantations and came instead from the back country and border areas. Hungry for better opportunities or pressed to move, they turned toward Missouri rather than the region north of the Ohio River which forbade slavery. These newcomers were well-acquainted with the Jeffersonian warnings against intrusive government and lavish public expenditures. Southern immigrants also carried a devotion to the Methodist and Baptist faiths, denominations which preached a gospel of the individual reach for salvation while also paradoxically prompting believers to distrust cultural novelty and political philosophies different from their own. Former Kentuckians and Tennesseans, for instance, took delight in their own frolicsome revivals and were alarmed at the casual way the Creole Missourians seemed to treat their Roman Catholic faith and the even lighter manner in which they approached the Sabbath.

Consequently, the new Missourians from the South combined a personal aggressiveness with a resentment of habits and ideas which they deemed frivolous or pernicious. This combination produced a code for personal conduct which many Protestants entering Missouri were determined to enforce—at least upon communicants. Records from Missouri's early days tell of church trials for Sabbath breaking, immorality, and dishonesty and of citizens often arrested for being profane or for gambling. The Missourians who concurred in this system were obviously very guarded in their approach to the relationship between individual freedom and social responsibility. For them liberty was a most delicate creature which ought not to be extended casually beyond such matters as separation of church and state, low taxes, and hard work.

Nineteenth-century events usually confirmed the southerner's cautious outlook. One result was that when the state established the first public university west of the Mississippi in 1839, the southern-dominated legislature refused for many years to appropriate money for it. There was supposed to be reassurance in the calling of James Shannon from a Kentucky college as the university's second president. Shannon was not simply an advocate of slavery: he was also a clergyman who chose to speak throughout Missouri in order to display religious evidence justifying Negro bondage. Shannon, it must be reported, proved too much even for Missouri to endure in the dual role of preacher and educator. However, an outlook which could mingle slavery, religion, and restrained society remained a volatile and enduring force in the state's public affairs. Carried into Missouri mostly by southerners, its presence lingered into the 1970s.

In addition to their colorful blend of individualism and conservatism, the Missourians with southern backgrounds brought another important contribution to the state's population. This was the Negro who, whether slave or free, was early an important figure among the many Missourians. The bitter anachronism of chattel bondage in America was nowhere better illustrated than in Missouri, where orators were pleased to stress how individual freedom and an equalitarian society prevailed. When other Missourians, especially those from Germany, began to point out that slavery contradicted the ideal of individual freedom, the black man's status became an uncommonly disputed subject. The slave was more important to Missouri's emotional history than to her economic story.

Most of the enslaved Missourians were found in the river valley counties, and especially across Little Dixie. In Howard County slaves made up 36 percent of the population in 1860. By that time the chattel system had moved westward along the Missouri River and into northeastern and northwestern quarters of the state, with the value of slaves apparently increasing significantly. A good field hand in 1830 cost $450, and in the late 1850s the price was as much as $1,500. The governor of Missouri estimated in 1860 that the value of the state's enslaved population was a hundred million dollars. Yet while the subject of slavery created an enormous furor in Missouri, only one slave state, Delaware, had a smaller percentage of slaves in its total population. Between 1820 and 1860, the proportion of bondsmen shrank in Missouri's populace from 20 percent to less than 10 percent. Under 3 percent of America's slave population was in Missouri, although such statistics could hardly comfort those actually in chains.

Slavery in Missouri followed a code patterned on the system used in Virginia, but there were differences in Missouri slavery and the kind practiced in more distinctly southern states. Missouri never officially defined slavery or indicated that only members of the black race were enslaved, and slaves worked differently from the blacks in field gangs on plantations in southern states. In fact, slaves in Missouri had jury trial rights and could sue for freedom if they could demonstrate they were being held illegally—a right of which some availed themselves successfully. However, such cases were rare, since the law took pains to forbid a black from testifying against whites. Manumission laws were apparently little used, and in 1847 a ban against teaching slaves to read or write was enacted.

As was true in America generally, segregation intensified in Missouri after 1875. Before that point, black Missourians were certainly considered an inferior part of society, but they associated freely with the white community. No less an authority than William G. Eliot, the St. Louis spiritual and educational leader who assuredly was no friend of bondage, acknowledged that slave treatment in Missouri seemed unusually humane. As such, it fed upon the kindness inherent in a paternalistic arrangement. Eliot was quick to add, however, that there were horrid exceptions to this strained benevolence.

The free Negroes in Missouri faced restrictive statutes and a hostile atmosphere nearly everywhere, reflecting the controversy surrounding admission as well as the usual talk of freedmen unsettling the chattel condition of most blacks. By 1847, free blacks were even more explictly forbidden to enter the state. Those who somehow had managed to become inhabitants—and there were about 3,500 free blacks in Missouri in 1860—were obliged to have licenses from the appropriate county court. In some areas these blacks had to provide bond assuring their proper behavior. However, an important free Negro community in St. Louis included members with significant amounts of property. Others succeeded as barbers, carpenters, nurses, and blacksmiths. Nevertheless, in the face of John Brown's raid in Virginia and the rising abolitionist cries, a near-hysterical Missouri legislature in 1859 enacted a statute ordering all free blacks between the ages of 18 and 35 who had entered the state since 1847 to depart at once. Those who refused would be sold by local sheriffs. Gov. Robert M. Stewart vetoed the bill on the ground that enforcement of existing legislation would serve the purpose.

Controversy in Missouri over the Negro deepened as the state's population grew more complex. Missouri had welcomed southerners with their black servants, but had also greeted other groups of new citizens whose views sharply differed from those of slaveowners. These newcomers, mostly from Germany and

New England, were outraged not only that Missouri permitted black bondage, but that northern states could accuse Missouri of being a breeding place for slaves to be shipped farther south. However, it was not easy in Missouri to oppose slavery openly. There was the celebrated fate of Elijah P. Lovejoy, who left a venerable New England family to come to St. Louis, where he published a paper critical of slavery and Roman Catholicism. In 1836, after a mob had burned a mulatto to death, a St. Louis judge ordered the culprits exonerated on the ground that Lovejoy's inflammatory articles had rendered them temporarily insane.

Lovejoy was driven to Illinois where his tactics in nearby Alton soon brought him a martyr's death. Meanwhile, the sentiment in Missouri after 1837 grew more bitter toward anything hinting of abolitionism. The growing German and New England population usually had to be content with supporting talk of creating a colony somewhere for blacks and with campaigning against opening any new territory west of the Mississippi to slavery. All of this scarcely promised a generous attitude toward black Missourians after the Civil War finally freed the slaves.

Emancipation brought no miraculous adjustment in Missouri's degradation of Negroes, whose lot continued to be difficult, especially in central and southern parts of the state. Even St. Louis was remarkably harsh. In 1870, for instance, the city chose to fight the evil of venereal disease by treating female prostitutes, the only cause of the problem which then could be publicly cited. In establishing a hospital for diseased prostitutes, the men in charge took care that Negro women were confined separately in the hospital basement. After 1870, in some parts of the state sheet clad Klansmen demonstrated their determination that Missouri must be kept safe through white supremacy while lynchings of blacks took place even as late as the 1930s. Segregation quickly became the way of life, marked especially by the establishment in 1875 of separate schools for blacks and whites, a practice which the next constitution of 1945 reaffirmed and which was not repealed until 1976.

Generally progress among Missouri blacks toward the franchise and educational opportunity was slow, although in some

respects faster than in other former slave states, thanks in part to
the helpful tone of the 1865 constitution. When the federal Constitution was amended to award suffrage to blacks, Missouri
seemed to accept it readily, and attempts at the close of the century to hamper Negro voting were not widely successful. Missouri came out of the Reconstruction era with the principle that
both black and white children should have the opportunity for
education, but since Missouri's public schools for whites were
vitiated by poor funding and anti-intellectualism, those for
blacks were even worse. It was this contrast between black and
white education that forced a brilliant young black named
George Washington Carver, born a slave in 1864, to leave Missouri. He went first to Kansas and then to Iowa for his school-
ing, and thereafter achieved international acclaim for his contributions in agricultural research. When Harry S. Truman
became president, six-year-old white and black children in his
beloved home town of Independence still trotted off to begin
their education in separate schools. When Truman returned to
Independence in 1953 after his administration, no black man or
woman fortunate enough to have completed high school could
normally be admitted to the University of Missouri.

There was a singular timeliness in the establishment in 1953
of the George Washington Carver National Monument in New-
ton County, where the distinguished scientist had been born.
Twenty years later, America recognized another Missouri black
emigré when in 1973 the public delightedly discovered Scott
Joplin's ragtime melodies, which he first composed and per-
formed in Sedalia brothels, the place in 1900 where Missouri
would most readily permit a black to be an entertainer. Missouri
had not been a hospitable place for blacks when Carver and
Joplin were growing up. Most of Missouri's black citizens,
young or old, had to await the mid-twentieth-century national
revolution in civil rights before Missouri's whites began accepting them as equal participants in the state's affairs.

The relationship between Negroes and whites appeared more
comfortable in Missouri than in some states, and racial friction
attracted less notice because of the small number of blacks in
the state. There were few "whites only" signs to be seen. Yet

segregation did exist. Blacks knew well they occupied an inferior position and that restaurants, restrooms, and other public facilities were not available to all Missourians on the same basis. The state's acceptance of segregation may have been subtle, but it was there all the same. When the oppression of blacks in America began to be eased, Missouri tended to accept the trend matter-of-factly. By 1970 the University of Missouri was struggling earnestly to attract and keep black students and faculty members. It was a new policy that would still have difficulty in the face of Missouri's long career in discrimination.

While Missouri's blacks were compelled to stand by themselves, another segment of the state's remarkably diverse population was eager for a time to emphasize its own difference: the body of Germans who came in great numbers between 1830 and 1860. Their legacy lingers in towns and villages with names such as Dutzow, Augusta, Altenburg, New Melle, Hermann, Westphalia, Wittenberg, and Frohna. These communities grew from a determination of the immigrants to remain united and to preserve beloved aspects of German life. The location of some of these old settlements now makes twentieth-century visitors shake their heads. Rocky hillsides and river bluffs with unpromising soil, so reminiscent of their native land, were usually selected by the Germans rather than the meadowlands which were then equally available.

On these comparatively wretched agricultural locations, German farmers applied Europe's centuries-old skills to transform barren and stubborn land into the abundant, carefully cultivated fields. In years preceding the Civil War, many Missouri agriculturists were known as "Latin Farmers," Germans comparatively well-educated in the classics who combined intellectual pursuits with farming. Even some of these learned farmers were forced to abandon the meager hills in disgust for life in St. Louis because of the unproductivity of the soil. On the whole, however, German diligence, enterprise, and family cohesion were important contributions to a frontier state where many citizens lacked such characteristics. These German qualities, along with other social and intellectual enrichments, did much toward shaping Missouri's spirit.

Missouri received most of the Germans in two phases. The first delegation, coming largely in the 1830s, consisted primarily of group or collective migration while, by the late 1840s, individual immigration was predominant. In both respects, however, the Germans arrived at what was then considered the far edge of American civilization, bringing a determination and hope more profound than those of many new Missourians from the South or the Ohio valley. For the American pioneers, removal westward was something an individual or family often experienced several times in life. Most German settlers found America and Missouri not just another more promising home, but a place where a new Germany might be established on the basis of cherished and often besieged ideals. For many Missouri Germans, their new location resembled what Cape Cod or the Schuylkill valley had meant two centuries earlier to Puritans and Quakers.

The vision of Missouri as a "New Germany" was glimpsed by numerous readers of Gottfried Duden's exhilarating descriptions of what might be attained along the Missouri River. Duden forsaw a second Eden of thriving agriculture, and did not anticipate the contribution of Germans in an urban setting like St. Louis. Instead, there were stirring early attempts to create isolated German communities in Missouri's limitless expanse. This group effort had been especially attractive to numerous Germans who were alarmed by the abortive outcome of their homeland's so-called revolutions of 1832 and 1833. The hazards of corporate emigration had always been enormous, and the group enterprise of these Germans proved no exception. For instance, the Geissen Emigration Society, established by Frederich Muench and Paul Follenius in 1833, had support in many parts of Germany. Yet disease and financial distress stalked the two groups of Geissen colonists who came to Missouri in 1834, forcing the society to dissolve and leaving the survivors to become struggling pioneers. Muench himself took a farm next to the land Duden had chosen when he lived in Warren County.

The limited communal success did not hinder the German immigrants from becoming a profound presence in several parts of Missouri. The remnant from the German Settlement Society of

Philadelphia, for example, created in 1839 the town of Hermann, a community which preserved German traditions with special skill throughout the nineteenth and twentieth centuries. Also in 1839 arrived some Germans from Saxony who were to become famous for their conservative Protestantism. This colony, which at first struggled around the village of Altenburg, eventually survived to found in 1847 the Lutheran Church, Missouri Synod, one of the most renowned German religious groups in America. Its outlook was so profoundly restrained that it was remarkable even for Missouri.

Anyone in the 1970s who wishes to recall those days of determined German Protestantism in Missouri would do well to seek out a small schoolhouse that still stands in the village of Femme Osage. The stones in this structure once made a church for Germans who had moved halfway around the world to arrive amidst the Boones and other American families in the beautiful countryside shared by Warren and St. Charles counties. Long abandoned, this old building and the graves surrounding it impart something of the durability of these Germans who brought their Evangelical faith and their determination to take up farming near Femme Osage, Dutzow, Marthasville, and New Melle. After a hundred and fifty years, evidence remained that Duden's dream had been more than fleeting. Flourishing farms, dwellings, customs, and family names on cemetery stones remain as tributes to men such as John H. and John F. Bierbaum who provided spiritual and practical leadership, so that many fellow Germans around Femme Osage became gradually just a part of Missouri.

By the time of the 1848 European upheavals, Germans began coming to Missouri mostly as individuals. Political pressures and economic distress made many of them anticipate civil and intellectual refuge in Missouri, as their predecessors in the 1830s had more often sought religious emancipation. During the 1850s, St. Louis received Germans who were teachers, lawyers, doctors, clergymen, and musicians. The latter especially made a rich contribution by encouraging an admiration for music which could be imparted perhaps only by disciples of Bach, Mozart, and Beethoven. Already by 1850, one out of three St. Louis citizens had been born in Germany so that in 1860, St. Louis had 50,510 German residents, many of whom were highly intelligent and well-trained advocates of their viewpoints. Of the foreign-born Missourians, over half were from Germany.

Two of the most notable among these newcomers were Dr. Emil Preetorius and Henry A. Brokmeyer. The former was a brilliant success as a St. Louis journalist, founding in 1862 *Die Neue Zeit,* which was the organ for German intellectuals. In 1864 he began publishing the *Westliche Post,* which had a long success. Typical of many Missouri Germans, Preetorius advocated perpetuating Germanism as well as the rising liberal-Republican viewpoint. Gradually the former mood disappeared as those who fled to Missouri around 1848 aged and died, so that when, in 1879, a German was elected head of the vital St. Louis Merchant's Exchange, amalgamation became evident. Soon St. Louis Germans became mayors, state officials, and even federal cabinet members. Preetorius himself was borne to his grave in 1905 by the governor of Missouri, former governors, the mayor, and assorted senators.

Possibly the most remarkable German to come to Missouri was Henry C. Brokmeyer, who gave part of his life to thoughtful primitivism in Warren County and another portion as philosophical leader for St. Louis. Possessing astonishing mental powers, Brokmeyer undertook nothing less than the task of enlarging upon the formidable ideas of G. W. F. Hegel, the dominant European philosopher, and of translating his *Logik.* In addition to speaking many Indian languages, Brokmeyer could also converse with Missouri politicians, so that this philosopher-statesman eventually served as lieutenant governor and acting governor, thus giving Missouri one of America's most amazing state executives. However, Brokmeyer joined many other Missouri politicians, apparently, in yielding to temptations offered by the railroad lobbies. This compromise brought his downfall, which drove him to become a hermit.

The careers of Preetorius and Brokmeyer, joined by those of Joseph Pulitzer and Carl Schurz, lend authority to the claim that beginning in the 1860s, German energy ruled St. Louis for a generation. Gradually, however, the Germans became old stock while their location remained quite regional, confined largely to St. Louis, to the Missouri and Mississippi River valleys, and to the hills bordering the Ozark region. Perhaps because of their dedication to disciplined work, their special customs, and their stout defense of cherished viewpoints, the Germans were controversial for nearly a century in all these locales.

In the 1850s fears were expressed that the immigration of Germans meant Missouri was being invaded by socialists and anarchists. In addition, the German loyalty to the free-soil and antislavery movements caused much resentment among neighbors with southern sympathies. Thanks to the Germans, Frank Blair and other leaders had the crucial support required to thwart Gov. Claiborne Jackson's attempt to lead Missouri out of the Union in 1861. Later the German unpopularity was reinforced by their opposition to the embittered reconstruction policies of Sen. Charles Daniel Drake and for their support of black civil rights. When the antisaloon forces began marching in the 1880s, the Germans rose stoutly to defend their cherished *biergartens*. Consequently, St. Louis remained a bastion for the "wets" until overwhelmed by national Prohibition.

Both in St. Louis and across the Missouri River valley, hostility toward the Germans was renewed after 1916 when the United States drifted into war with Germany. There was more than international politics involved as neighbors with German names and ancestry were intimidated and mistreated, despite the fact that many Missourians of German ancestry joined the United States armed services. In St. Louis there was even talk of segregating the Germans. Berlin Avenue was renamed after Missouri's son, Gen. John J. Pershing, who led the American military expedition to France. Despite the caustic rebuke of editor Reedy in his *Mirror,* the talk of denying Germans the use of many streets and bridges persisted. Attempts were made outstate to discourage using the German language in church services.

The animosity worsened when many Missourians with German backgrounds spoke against what they claimed was the rise of militarism in the United States. As the war began, stories circulated that food served in German restaurants held secret potions aimed at slackening the patriotism of unsuspecting patrons. The teaching of German in many high schools was challenged, along with the motives of many of those who published German-American newspapers, while many German-owned businesses felt compelled to purchase newspaper space to advertise how they endorsed the Allied cause. Despite the fact that the German place in Missouri's culture was almost as old as the state itself, the capitulation of some citizens to the anti-German hysteria during World War I destroyed many venerable friendships and associations among Missourians.

Much less evident than the German immigration was the early arrival in Missouri of still another group. These were the newcomers from New England, many of whom had lived in the Ohio River valley before crossing into Missouri. While these Yankees grew especially important during and after the Civil War, they significantly affected Missouri's outlook even earlier since the population with a northeastern background had increased by nearly 200 percent in the 1850s. These Missourians, when linked with the Germans, soon outnumbered those with a southern heritage. The New Englanders brought more than a natural reserve. From them, primarily, came the push in Missouri toward commerce and industry. However, the furor over slavery, territorial status, and state rights also claimed their interest.

Some Missourians, especially those on the state's western rim, considered a New Englander to be instinctively bent upon trouble, as the controversial career of the New England Aid Society seemed to prove. This organization, which grew from the Massachusetts Emigrant Aid Society, had vowed that regions adjacent to Missouri must be settled by men opposed to slavery. Although the actual effect of the group was much less than many citizens supposed, the activity of those in the society accomplished two things. It deepened the suspicion in agricultural circles that a Yankee newcomer was dangerously meddlesome and different; and it suggested to the New Englanders that their adopted state might need more than coaxing to continue as a dynamic part of the Union.

For a century after the Civil War, the frustrations lingered as many Yankees—or those who assumed eastern airs—endured the dominance of Missouri's deepening rural caution. Such a feeling stimulated the movement for home rule and separate status for St. Louis and lay behind the determination of many families, especially in the state's metropolitan areas, to send their children to schools and colleges along the Atlantic seaboard. Nor did eastern America forget Missouri. To look after his family's sizeable investments in Missouri, Charles Francis Adams II dispatched his son, John Quincy Adams, great-grandson of President J. Q. Adams, to take up life in Kansas City around the turn of the century. This move mirrored the mingled guardianship and misgiving felt toward Missouri by many northeasterners, whether they lived in the state or watched from afar. Actually, old Charles F. Adams himself continued to visit Missouri regularly hoping to remedy personally what he felt was the lack of wisdom and imagination in native Missourians.

The caution and restraint which bothered the Adamses and which increasingly characterized Missouri after 1875 was often blamed on the departure of many promising citizens. This exodus accompanied the relative decline in the state's growth rate. In her first half-century, Missouri did attract such invigorating figures as John Hiram Lathrop, first president of the struggling University of Missouri and others such as Thomas Hart Benton, Edward Bates, Paul Follenius, William G. Eliot, and Frank Blair. With this flow of leaders reversed in the last quarter of the nineteenth century, Missouri became a fertile producer of talent to enrich other states. Certainly, few worthy replacements were evident for Carl Schurz, Joseph Pulitzer, William T. Harris, Samuel Clemens, and George Washington Carver. With these and other emigrants went much of Missouri's chance for regaining the position of leadership she held in the Union in the 1830s, a time marked by the belief that Missouri's mix of dynamic people had brought forth a man worthy to succeed Jefferson and Jackson in leading America. His name was Thomas Hart Benton.

6

Jeffersonian Missouri: Benton's Era

*T*HE newcomers flocking into Missouri after 1821 found that admission to the Union had by no means ended political debate. Instead, the state was soon launched on a course which, with rare exception, remained dedicated to the ideals of Thomas Jefferson. From her early days, Missouri appeared determined to acknowledge public goals that many other states came to regard as unrealistic or antiquated. Although she reached statehood in a period of national political confusion, Missouri quickly took to reminding America of old economic and social virtues. Even if the state represented the forward thrust of America's frontier expansion, she preferred to turn back to familiar preachments about limited government, agrarianism, and the dangers of money and banking. When she created a town as her capital in 1821, Missouri naturally named it Jefferson. One hundred and fifty years later an especially appropriate gesture by Missourians for the bicentennial season had the University of Missouri moving its most revered possession, the stone monument originally marking Jefferson's grave at Monticello, to a location of greater prominence and beauty on its Columbia campus. The tombstone had been given to the university by Jefferson's descendants.

Missouri's public outlook seemed to assume that America needed help in building the society which the Jeffersonians praised. Most other western states had similar intentions, but few would match the steadfastness of Missouri, where for many citizens the simplifications in the Jeffersonian philosophy came to have a peculiar charm. There was general agreement among Missourians that the hope of America lay in free citizens immune to coercion as a result of their widespread ownership of the land. Such freedom, Missourians tended to argue, required a society relying upon subsistence agriculture. Out of this perspective, banks with their deceitful paper money and towns with their wage slaves appeared to most Missourians to be the way an unwitting population became chained to privilege and eventually to corruption.

All these ideas became grist ground in the mills of Missouri's successful orators. They relied especially upon the writings of Jefferson's great disciples, Nathaniel Macon and John Taylor, who carried to the limit the refrain that government was best when it functioned least. For Macon, for Taylor, and for generations of Missourians, the paradox of good government was that it ought to take every precaution to see that no one betrayed the farmer's independence. From this staunch belief most Missourians came to dread taxes, banks, paper money, sophisticated commerce, and city influences. On the other hand, they predicted that Missouri was where the old forces of greed, corruption, tyranny, poverty, and the degradation of city life might be overcome. The crucial requirement, of course, was the independence and inspiration brought by fresh natural surroundings.

Generally there was little quarrel in early Missouri with these simplifications. Avowed foes of Jeffersonian doctrine were scarce west of the Mississippi. In 1828 Missouri began her famed loyalty to the Democratic party by acclaiming Andrew Jackson as the one who had been summoned from the Tennessee wilderness to defend the old agrarian values. Nevertheless, while political differences in Missouri tended to be more a matter of degree than of kind, there were to be sharp controversies. Missouri was often the setting for battles over city and farm influence, over authority distributed between executive and legislative branches of government, over the use of tax power and the revenue itself, and over the extent to which technology and education were safe social tools. All these were common disputes in most states, but such issues had a special poignancy in Missouri. The events of her history kindled in Missouri an often blind devotion to the simpler world for which Jefferson had seemed the great defender. Frequently disappointed and divided within, Missouri grew increasingly cautious and even paranoid, for as she watched, her hopes for an America of naturally wise and sturdily independent farmers were destroyed by progress.

At the outset, Missouri's Jeffersonians found a splendid target. They assailed the junto, as it was called—a group of politicians in St. Louis who were accustomed to dominating territorial affairs. Members of the clique were drawn from the men of wealth and business, the land speculators, the lawyers, and the few aristocrats who came from the long-established French families. The junto's most serious misstep was to favor confirmation of the numerous and generous land grants left by Spain. This was a distinctly unpopular prospect beyond St. Louis in areas where the newer settlers had brought with them memories of earlier fights against plutocrats who had taken advantage of being first on the scene.

When the state's constitution was prepared in 1820, the authors were mostly junto men—educated and prosperous landholders, lawyers, doctors, and businessmen. Consequently, the convention's failure to submit its work to a popular referendum, the contents of the constitution itself, and the identity of the framers all became issues in the elections held later in 1820 for governor and for members of the first general assembly. The results confounded the junto and shaped the future for Missouri politicians. What most alarmed many voters was that the new constitution seemed to call for an independent judiciary to curb the popularly chosen legislature. This provision smacked of real evil since Missourians well knew how Jefferson's old foe, Chief Justice John Marshall, had talked of the threat to order and progress if capricious state assemblies were not restrained by judicial review. A few convention members led by Alexander McNair argued in vain for limits on the court's capacity. Consequently, before the convention concluded, McNair announced that he would take the issue to the people and seek the governor's chair, despite the fact he would have to run against William Clark, whom the junto backed.

During the campaign, McNair deliberately sought rural support, mingling comfortably with types of citizens whom the city establishment avoided. He won handily, although the distinctions were vague and the issues by no means clear. The victors in Missouri's first general election were markedly of a Jeffersonian character. Quickly thereafter, the rising political power outside of St. Louis became organized while it also sought to simplify the questions facing nation and state. In this fragile setting Missouri developed some of her enduring social and economic prejudices, while Jefferson's heirs tried to learn how best to manage Missouri.

As an initial step the first general assembly undertook to cleanse the constitution of what many persons considered its undemocratic character. Most legislators believed that the general assembly should be made dominant in public affairs, with the result that amendments were passed which granted legislators power to appoint judges and certain administrative officials. Constitutionally prescribed minimum salaries for judges and governors were put aside in the belief that the reward of public officials should regularly be set by the people's spokesmen. Since proposed amendments had to await the election of another legislature for final adoption, new considerations arising from economic depression had taken the stage by 1822, leaving the next general assembly the time and interest to confirm only a few of the amendments.

Constitutional alarm gave way to other issues which proved perhaps even more suitable for Jeffersonian agitation. These questions clustered around the economic depression which arrived after 1820 from the beleaguered East to assail the new state. With debt widespread, a confused and youthful legislature sinned briefly but mightily in the eyes of Jeffersonian orthodoxy by attempting to aid the public through issuing relief notes which would circulate as paper money. Before slavery split Missouri, no issue more clearly revealed the state's philosophy than the debates over the proper form of money. Followers of Jefferson and Jackson considered money coined from gold or silver as the rock upon which a righteous society must be built. They stressed the merit of such coins, often called specie or hard money, in contrast to paper money. For them the circulation of paper notes by banks or government as a substitute for gold or silver coins promised dreadful results. Whereas hard money, coined by the people's government out of bullion, supposedly had absolute value, paper money, it was alleged, created false hopes and was subject to deceitful practice since such currency was no better than the capacity of the originators to redeem it in specie.

Missourians with Jeffersonian leanings therefore listened sympathetically to warnings that wealthy and greedy men would use banks or government to circulate paper money in order to drive up prices, stimulate debt, and thus enrich themselves. When this happened, the argument ran, farmers and workers became prisoners of a false monetary system founded on private greed and not on the indisputable presence of bullion. Meanwhile, depression experiences after 1821 were so startling and severe as to dampen the optimism which earlier had brought many Missourians to behave as if their new state's position and resources made any economic gamble, including reliance on paper money, worthwhile. A brief investment frenzy followed by collapsed prices resulted in much genuine suffering across Missouri, prompting devastated citizens who thought their debts were hopeless to ask for help from the state. Believing momentarily that something could be paid for with nothing, the general assembly not only granted debt-ridden Missourians additional time to meet their obligations, but it also issued certificates of loan which were to circulate as money while retiring debts. However, confusion, faulty legislation, and judicial opposition brought this exercise in public aid to an unhappy conclusion; its major result was that it strengthened the prejudices of many Missourians against active government and use of paper money.

Rising caution led many Missourians to be quick in fixing blame for their economic plight on the banks and the seductively easy money they made available, but those who castigated the banks overlooked the haste with which settlers had grabbed the chance for credit in more optimistic times. Looking back from 1822, many saddened citizens confessed that by using the banks they had trafficked with representatives of the evil against which Jeffersonians had inveighed. Two banks had been chartered by the territorial government. Although the Bank of St. Louis and the Bank of Missouri failed in 1819 and 1821, respectively, their story touched the outlook of Missourians for generations. It was easy for many citizens to blame a false and malicious boom on the banks' distribution of paper notes. The territory had permitted these notes to circulate as paper money to supplement the rare Spanish coins and the barter method on which most Missourians depended. When the banks failed, their paper notes or "money" proved worthless to the citizens who had collected them as a means of paying their debts. The banks' use of paper notes thus seemed to many citizens to have been false encouragement and proof of how the rich preyed upon the poor. Seventeen years passed before Missouri again permitted a bank within her borders, and when she did, she filled its charter with elaborate restrictions.

For a generation after 1820, Missouri was divided into two hostile camps. The forces demanding only coined money were called "hards." Normally a majority, they also stood for restraining the energy of government. Dissenters, named "softs," believed that banks and government must stimulate economic and social growth through such inducements as a generous circulation of paper money. For the "softs," progress in Missouri would come only if the economy relied on more than the limited supply of gold and silver. "Hards" believed that bankers, lawyers, speculators, merchants, and especially the government must not interfere with the wholesome order of a simple economy. The quarrel between these protagonists dominated public affairs in Missouri for many years and its enduring marks included a deepened caution about using tax money for education, roads, and aid to the poor. Missourians came to display an almost pathological suspicion of taxes, banks, and commerce.

This ordeal also prepared Missouri to speak strongly in national politics in behalf of Andrew Jackson, who had become president of the United States in 1829. The hero from Tennessee and his Democratic party appeared to a majority of Missourians by 1830 as the most likely to restore the hopes that Jefferson had held for the Republic. Jackson's rhetoric about self-help and the prizing of localism had a soothing and even unifying quality in most parts of the state, except St. Louis. As other states contrived policies to develop transportation and business, Missouri stood aside in lonely dignity. The experience of ten years earlier with banks and relief legislation was enough to remind citizens that progress could never come by compromising Jeffersonian ideals. The popularity Henry Clay once had in Missouri was gone by 1832. His advocacy of such vigorous public steps as national banking, protective tariffs, and public construction of roads and canals had a following limited to business interests in St. Louis.

This is not to say that most Missourians had no wish for the blessings of roads, money, and high prices. What frightened them were the penalties as described by the Jacksonians in traditional Jeffersonian terms—a power-hungry government run by free-spending and selfish bankers, businessmen, lawyers, and landed aristocrats. Consequently, by 1832 Jackson's cloudy views on national needs had drawn 70 percent of Missouri's eligible voters into the Democratic party. Thereafter, and into the last half of the twentieth century, Missouri usually stood with the Democrats, especially when the party chose to espouse good Jeffersonian doctrine. Here was the clue to the success of the two Missourians most important in federal councils, Thomas Hart Benton and Harry S. Truman. As pure as disciples of Jefferson could hope to be, these two men were beloved in Missouri for their strenuous campaigns in behalf of one who came to be known as "the little man." They found ways to be successful in the often necessarily negative task of crusading against power and wealth, whether in public or private hands.

Other Missouri figures were normally less skillful or lucky. Missouri's earnest regard for Jeffersonian values doomed most of her spokesmen in national affairs to undistinguished careers. For a century and a half, few Missouri congressmen and senators managed to make a positive force out of Missouri's inherently negative outlook, a failure leaving most of them appearing obstructionist, self-serving, and even absurd. Benton and Truman each found the genius to elude this usual graveyard of Missouri politicians. The case of Thomas Hart Benton was especially revealing since his career as a Missouri leader in the nation was so lengthy. Eventually, the implacable pressures of changing circumstances overcame Benton, but not before this mighty Missourian had proven a master in drawing appealing themes from the creeds of Jefferson and Jackson. Benton's career and viewpoints offer the key to understanding Missouri's time of strength in national affairs.

Thomas Hart Benton was one of numerous Missourians who lived uneasily with his past. He never quite forgot his embarrassing student days at the University of North Carolina which had ended in charges of stealing. Nor, in turn, could he escape recalling the hot-tempered defenses of his honor which drove him to commit murder on the dueling field. Benton's most vivid memory, however, was of his pilgrimage to Monticello on Christmas Eve in 1824 and conversations there with the aged Thomas Jefferson. For Benton, the Jeffersonian tradition became an obsession, even prompting his reconciliation with Andrew Jackson although the two men once had a violent encounter back in Tennessee. Jackson's devotion to Jeffersonian ideals was reason enough for Benton to be forgiving. Missouri was especially important to Benton for there he believed nature's favors most assured an ideal republic of sturdy farmers.

Benton reached St. Louis in 1815 at age 33. He brought with him an uneven but successful record of public service in Tennessee, where he had displayed an early respect for cheap land and hard money. For a time Benton groped toward a rewarding place in Missouri affairs, appearing at first to be a lackey for French aristocrats and the St. Louis junto. He also did more than his share to persuade older states that Missouri Territory prized violence. In one of America's most ghastly duels, Benton slew Charles Lucas, the scion of a prominent St. Louis family. Accepting a challenge in 1817 arising from factional rivalry, Benton said his honor was unsatisfied when a first encounter on "Bloody Isle" in the Mississippi River proved inconclusive. Spurred by local gossip, he demanded a second meeting in which he deliberately killed young Lucas. True, only the prominence of the combatants made this event conspicuous around St. Louis, but to more distant observers Benton had sensationally illustrated the irrational fury which appeared to characterize Missouri politics.

Benton drew nearer to success when he discovered that public affairs in Missouri had moved beyond personal competition among St. Louis power brokers, all dominated by an elitist outlook. Benton's nimbleness after 1820 carried him above the taint of St. Louis associations to a union with the farmers of Missouri's hinterland. This combination was remarkable since as late as 1819 Benton had been using the newspapers to offer Missouri his platform for a new state's well-being, a stand with no denunciation of business exploitation or the prospect of federal aid. However, when this viewpoint almost cost him election as one of Missouri's first United States senators, a surprised Benton recognized the dangers of a link with city politics. At the same time he was quick to appreciate that joining the rising rural power beyond St. Louis meant giving precedence to his latent Jeffersonian philosophy. To excuse the fact, at least, that the St. Louis junto had made his first election to the federal Senate possible, Benton hastened to remind people that Daniel Boone's son, Jesse, had nominated him before the general assembly. In this faltering fashion, at age thirty-eight, Benton thus began his national career while Missouri herself sought to emerge from her own political uncertainties. Only briefly had Benton shared the views of his distant kinsman, Henry Clay, who believed in progress through federal encouragement for manufacturing and commerce. By 1825, Benton and his Missouri backers condemned Clay's position as old Federalism.

Benton's colleague from Missouri, Sen. David Barton, was a far more attractive and popular individual than Benton. Curiously, however, Barton was increasingly aligned with what many Missourians considered privilege and aristocratic government. While Benton bolted from the side of special interest and soon claimed to be leading the people in their ceaseless fight against wealth, Barton did not find public affairs to be quite so simple. Consequently, America watched the first two senators from Missouri drift apart, personally and philosophically. The two men rarely exchanged greeting, and Barton methodically opposed Benton's proposals, taking special pleasure in disputing the latter's plan for gradually reducing the price of all public land which had remained unsold for any time.

Until he chose not to seek re-election in 1830, David Barton moved farther afield from his state's emerging viewpoint. He insisted that Benton's denunciation of the energetic government which Adams and Clay called "the American System" would simply provoke class antagonisms and rouse a dangerous popular ire. To the end of his unhappy days, Barton repudiated the religion of popular rule and preferred to stand with men like Chief Justice John Marshall in arguing that good society in America required a strong federal government, a court system above the people's passion, and leadership from men proven fit to govern. In 1830 Barton left public life, retiring to die by alcoholism which had increasingly helped to blight his efforts at home and in Washington. By then, Barton's aristocratic views had been overwhelmed and men approached Benton with respect, recognizing that Jeffersonian philosophy had triumphed in Missouri in large part because of Benton's skill in tying it to the appeal of Andrew Jackson. Ironically, Barton remained a quiet, humble person while Benton grew more arrogant and imperious with the years.

Thereafter, both Missouri and Senator Benton displayed a fascinating political development. Missouri was soon dominated by the farmers and workingmen of the countryside and small towns who preferred to hear about cheap land, hard money, and simple government. There was much delight in Missouri, for instance, when Benton took as one of his first causes amending the federal Constitution to permit popular election of presidents. Nevertheless, though Benton's and Missouri's viewpoints might be faithful to Jacksonian democracy, the state's variety doomed the Democrats to perpetual fractiousness and ambivalence. The area most steadfast for the ideals of Jefferson's old Republic and the aspirations of Senator Benton was the Boonslick counties. Until the rupture over slavery, these Missouri river districts were Benton's mainstay. Aside from this region, however, the mixture of immigration and diverse local interests after 1830 made predictions about political behavior difficult.

Since Benton's alliance with Jackson made him by 1832 the president's chief spokesman, St. Louis was hardly a hospitable place. The town refused to abandon the fiscal policies associated with the Second Bank of the United States, disparagingly called "the Monster" by Bentonians. Increasingly, Benton had to count on the counties of small farmers, the areas rapidly becoming dominant in the state, to squelch the opposition from economically more sophisticated regions of Missouri. Events had an uncanny way of complying with Benton's preaching. At the three points when Missouri cautiously began encouraging banking, the national depressions of 1819, 1837, and 1857 swooped down upon the state as if to sanctify the warnings of Benton and his hard-money followers.

Benton himself was not always easy to comprehend. Often it seemed that he used Missouri merely as an electioneering base. His stays in St. Louis, purportedly his home, were intermittent, while the Benton family grew up largely amid relatives in Virginia and later preferred to live in Washington. However, when Missouri voters doubted him, Benton usually had a ready answer. In 1835 he was obliged to explain his enthusiasm over the executive energies of President Jackson when, a decade before, he had been warning against such an evil eventuality. Benton simply urged his followers to recognize that the end justified the means. The Jacksonian sword, Benton explained to Missouri's yeoman population, was cutting down enemies of an agrarian republic.

During these times, the 1820s and 1830s, Benton and his Missouri followers were hailed—or scorned—by national observers as radicals. This slippery term was attached to Benton's rising determination to defend a Jeffersonian America by selling public land at low prices and defeating efforts to entice farmers into debt through the availability of paper money. As defender of hard cash, Benton soon earned his nickname, "Old Bullion," and a reputation as guarantor of an old order. Generally, Benton's massive influence in Missouri and the nation came to be used to preserve an old-fashioned pastoral society. His struggles against the wizards of finance and for cheap land were his most effective strategies. Through them he encouraged within Missourians their natural suspicions of big government, glamorous economic legislation, and urban viewpoints.

Benton's fame was as great as his impact on the spirit of caution that endured in Missouri. Missourians were proud in the 1830s that, less than a generation after statehood, their senator was widely suggested for the presidency. In many areas of the state it was confidently announced that Benton stood next to Vice-President Van Buren in the succession to President Jackson. The Missouri senator towered on the national scene, bringing an especially thrilling moment to his admiring constituents when he fought to expunge from the United States Senate record the censure of President Jackson for practicing Jeffersonian economics. It was natural that Benton should be chosen in 1837 to obliterate the condemnation of Jackson's fight for hard money which the Whigs had managed to get into the Senate journal. Jackson himself gave the place of honor to Benton when the president was host to his own supporters at a dinner during the administration's waning moments.

When the depression worsened after 1837, it was Benton's Missouri, firm on the rock of fiscal conservatism, which appeared to be the only state faithful to the simple, rural commonwealth which Jefferson had urged and Jackson had echoed. As banks of other states were failing, the Bank of the State of Missouri thrived, with notes soundly based on specie reserves and bearing the portrait of Benton, whom America now acclaimed as the "Gibraltar of the West." Benton meanwhile continued to insist on the purest hard-money policies for Missouri, opposing any relief measures during economic pinch, thereby causing a rising uneasiness among some of his followers who wondered if "Old Bullion" might not be a bit unreasonable. Nevertheless, as late as 1842 every Missouri congressman was still a Benton man, illustrating how the senator's greatest moments in politics occurred in the decade following 1837. These years may also have been Missouri's most significant period in American public affairs.

A memorable evaluation of Benton was made by the brilliant Swedish commentator on America, Fredrika Bremer. Writing in 1850 after visiting the federal Senate, Miss Bremer called Benton "the hawk from Missouri" and contrasted his repute for cold-blooded courage in dueling with his being "widely esteemed for his learning." Miss Bremer thought this must be explained by Benton's Missouri origin, which meant he belonged "to that class which springs up on the outskirts of the wilderness and among a half-savage people." Calling Benton an appropriate spokesman for the region "where the wild Missouri pours its turbid waters along its perilous course," Bremer said "only half-civilized Missouri" would accept, from a representative, the pleasure in violence and the resolute determination that characterized Benton. The combination, in her view, made Benton "both esteemed and feared as a political character." [1]

In these wondrous years for Benton, President Jackson's shrewd adviser, Francis P. Blair, sent his sons, Montgomery and Frank, to St. Louis to work as the Missourian's protégés in politics and law. Even in St. Louis, support for Benton was rising. With these achievements, Benton was triumphantly reelected by the general assembly in 1838, after which he did a most uncharacteristic thing: he toured Missouri on horseback to thank the faithful who had stood with him for Jeffersonian principles. Ordinarily rather pompous and aloof, Benton actually talked with many citizens, repeatedly reminding them of how Missouri was alone in America as a state free of the fiscal and political evils in control elsewhere.

Benton also used his tour to urge that Missourians be mindful of their state's great natural blessings. He stressed especially the wonderful land still amply available in Missouri. Further liberalization of federal land legislation through pre-emption was the senator's next national goal. However, here began the great irony in Benton's career, and also much torment for Missouri. The very forces of agricultural growth which Benton fostered

1. Fredrika Bremer, *America of the Fifties: Letters of Fredrika Bremer*, ed. Adolph B. Benson (London: Oxford University Press, 1924), pp. 184–185. These letters were originally published in Swedish in 1853.

MISSOURI

A photographer's essay by A. Y. Owen

Photographs in sequence

Cattle farm near Seneca.
Showboat and river barge on the Mississippi River at St. Louis.
Missouri River at Kansas City.
Gateway Arch, St. Louis.
Aging wine in wooden casks near Hermann.
Banks of the Mississippi River, Hannibal.
From corncobs to corncob pipes, Washington.
Covered bridge and gristmill, Burfordville.
Meat store, New Hampton.
Old home, Chillicothe.
Farm near Ewing.
Delivering Saturday morning's mail in business district, Elsberry.
Noblett Lake, near Willow Springs.
Quarrying gray marble, Carthage.
Mennonite buggies and wagons at hitching post, Jamesport.

now started to vex him. As Missouri expanded, her economic character and needs grew more complex while the Democratic party became unwieldy from sheer size. The fate of a proposed constitution presented to Missouri voters in 1846 was instructive. This document was prepared by the state's second constitutional convention which had been called primarily out of two Jeffersonian concerns. These had been demands that newly populous areas should have more adequate representation and that the state's government should be better able to quash attempts by banks and business to corrode the public interest. The result, however, was an extremely reactionary document whose various shortcomings combined to discourage many supporters. The voters rejected the new charter, but not because of its opposition to powerful government and an encroaching commercial world.

Actually, these old preoccupations were being set aside in Missouri as efforts began in Washington to extend slavery's domain by annexing Texas, a development with the profoundest effect on both Benton and his state. President John Tyler's attempt to secure Texas for the Union obliged Benton to concentrate on opposing the extension of slavery and to urge the importance of the Union. For him these were principles as vigorous as any other part of Jefferson's creed. Neither the venerable Andrew Jackson, dying at the Hermitage, nor many of Benton's rural faithful in Missouri could agree that this new course was Jeffersonian orthodoxy. It dismayed Missourians to see Benton allied with his ancient foe, former President John Quincy Adams, upon the slavery question. This alarm was evident when Benton was hard pressed to win his last election to the Senate in 1844. Trouble was clearly ahead as rising Democrats in Missouri, such as Claiborne Fox Jackson and David R. Atchison, began opposing "Old Bullion." Agitation over an agrarian republic founded on hard money and cheap land, Benton's traditional issue, was not sufficient to distract Missourians from two revived issues: slavery, and federal restrictions that threatened new states.

Benton, however, refused to equivocate. He rejoiced in America's victory over Mexico, but added that slavery must not increase an inch because of those triumphs. Acknowledging the impending westward growth beyond Missouri, Benton somehow reconciled two positions which seemed impossible to many Missourians. On the one hand he became as ardent in behalf of railroad extension across the plains as, on the other side, he vehemently opposed the accompaniment of slavery alongside this development. Benton managed to convince himself that a mechanized improvement like a transcontinental railroad would not endanger the primacy of the small farmers or of simple government, but though he may have persuaded some Missourians not to fear the railroads, the senator was much less successful in raising support in Missouri against slavery expansion.

Many Missouri leaders found it easy to put aside for the moment the familiar attacks on conspiratorial wealth in order to assail the new specter—northern plots to harm slavery. Here was a version of government aggression against states which Missouri well rememberd in her own history and thus once more hastened to denounce, even though it required repudiating Benton. In March 1849, the general assembly took the plunge by passing resolutions which repeated the dogma taught by slavery's friends, resolutions bearing the name of their author, Claiborne F. Jackson. The legislature's action was aimed directly at Benton, for the Jackson Resolutions pointedly instructed Missouri's senators immedittely to begin opposing any congressional effort to hinder a territory's right to welcome slavery. The legislature even announced that recent aggression by northern states justified southern states in ignoring the Missouri Compromise's prohibition of slavery north of the 36°30′ line.

The Jackson Resolutions were intended to make a stir in Congress, and they succeeded. For Benton, who had long preached the importance for representatives to abide by instructions from their constituents, it was an awkward moment. He made it even more tense by pompously brushing aside the resolutions, saying they did not represent the views of Missouri's people, even though both houses of the general assembly had enthusiastically passed them. The old senator decided to prove to America that his real constituency, the Missouri "people" he loved to talk about, opposed unleashing slavery. In doing so he displayed political courage and tenacity that were unrivaled in the state's history until Harry Truman's efforts of a century later.

From May to November 1849, Benton stumped Missouri, speaking against slavery's expansion even in communities where growing hostility threatened his life. Everywhere he insisted he knew what the poeple really believed, which meant that they agreed with his stand on slavery. However, what even Benton did not perceive was that as his hold on rural Missouri slipped, St. Louis was becoming his chief sympathizer. Immigrants from Germany and Ireland did much to bolster the town's free-soil viewpoint. But it was all for nought. A year after the senator's famous trip around the state, the general assembly proceeded to elect a senator, struggling through forty ballots before ending Benton's brilliant career in the Senate on 22 January 1851.

At once began a new phase of Missouri politics as well as a new level of animosity between city and countryside. Men like Benton were now unable to hold a wide constituency by courageous—some thought neurotic—shouts that citizens who favored slavery and soft money were not worthy to be Missourians. Benton and Missouri were caught in the nation's widening plight wherein Jeffersonian orthodoxies no longer assured unity. Still, Benton refused to quit. At the age of seventy, "Old Bullion" seemed to hear hurrahs for the "Gibraltar of the West." He won a term in the federal House of Representatives, sitting for, of all places, the district including St. Louis. He said he was glad at last to be speaking directly for the people, but Benton had scant success in trying to be an interested spokesman for mercantile affairs, so his stay in the House was brief.

Thereafter, all that remained were glorious defeats. In the winter of 1854–1855, Benton's lingering supporters were able to block the election of another senator by denying a majority to anyone proposed in the general assembly. The Senate seat remained vacant for two years, a silent testimony to Missouri's deepening divisions. Appropriately, Benton stayed to the end one of the most earnest advocates of American unity. When his son-in-law, John Charles Frémont, was the Republican presidential candidate in 1856, Benton did not support him for fear his election would enlarge sectional hatred. After engineering the Democratic nomination of the pallid James Buchanan for president, Benton agreed to run for governor in Missouri. In that campaign, the old man spoke throughout the state to huge crowds who heard him stress the importance of harmony in the Republic. Yet even after talking to 10,000 citizens in St. Louis during an outdoor meeting, the "Gibraltar of the West" ran a poor third in the gubernatorial race.

Benton gave his remaining time to completion of a massive digest of congressional debates which he insisted contained the scriptural testimony for the great Jeffersonian legacy of both Missouri and the nation—a prescription, of course, for a democracy of small farmers rejoicing in free and cautious government amid natural abundance. So relentlessly did this vision grip Benton that somehow he refused to let cancer kill him until 10 April 1858, a few moments after he finally put down his pen. He bequeathed to Missouri a tradition which his beloved Democratic party would nurture for generations, once the slavery issue was gone. According to this legacy, it behooved all Missourians and their descendants to defend the admirable society where citizens lived in simplicity and independence amid nature's inspiration.

Missouri's history was to show, however, that sustaining this outlook took a heavy toll in public emotion as an atmosphere of dislike and mistrust developed among many Missourians amidst changing economic and political trends. Benton's heirs seemed naturally to be on guard against banks, taxes, and human nature. The costly tension from such a persisting Jeffersonian spirit was evident in Benton's era in a tragic way, bringing anguish to Benton's political ally, Gov. Thomas Reynolds, who had been elected in 1840 during an agonizing depression. While facing bitter personal assaults for his caution on such stirring topics as money, banking, debtor relief, and constitutional reform, Reynolds received the greatest invective when he opposed pressure to have the state try again to use paper money as an aid to indebtedness. Tormented by this abuse which a vocal minority created over his faithfulness in the Jeffersonian cause, Reynolds crumpled beneath the strain. Early in 1844 the governor of Missouri committed suicide, an exhausted champion of Benton's gospel.

While the attacks on Reynolds exposed the feelings stirred among Missourians by the conservative tradition, they also hinted at the deeper torment even then overtaking the state. Those who wished to defend slavery's right to be taken into new territories thus skillfully exploited Missouri's general uneasiness within America's development, obliging her to retire as a powerful force in the Union. Where once she had led in arousing the nation over the apostasies of enlarged federal government, rising business and banking influence, and growing cities, Missouri by 1855 had turned inward to face her own discord. The fates of Benton and Reynolds were instances of how new issues threatened the conditions and values which most Missourians had taken for granted not long before, sadly dividing the state.

7

Times of Torment

$\mathcal{T}$EN years after Missouri became a state, a band of settlers, believing that Missouri was a holy land, appeared in Jackson County. With the arrival of this advance party of the Church of Jesus Christ of Latter-day Saints, followers of Joseph Smith, Missouri began times of great torment. These Saints, often called Mormons, were eventually expelled following much brutality. Soon thereafter, bloody conflicts over the future of slavery broke out between Missouri and Kansas. Then came the appalling Civil War years in which Missouri's distress was beyond that of most other states in the Union or the Confederacy. After the North's victory, ten years of bitter controversy began over the character of a new Missouri. Finally, an era of lawlessness brought sections of Missouri into virtual anarchy. Order was restored in the 1880s, ending what had been fifty years of internal torment and leaving Missouri with terrible memories.

When the Mormons arrived in 1831, western Missouri seemed to embody America's future. With amazing swiftness, disciples of Joseph Smith and, later, followers of John Brown aroused intolerance and hatred in the area. Smith was certain that God had selected Jackson County as the place where the Saints could gather to await the holy summons. Independence thus became the Saints' Zion. Such a proprietary outlook unnerved or angered many other Jackson Countians who feared that the Saints' highly efficient organization would surely drive all others away. By 1833, one-third of Jackson County's population was Mormon. However, the area's first settlers had come mostly from the South. Living precariously on the edge of civilization and clinging to their slaves and to their beginnings in agriculture or commerce, these pioneer Missourians peered uneasily at the Mormons as well as at the Indians just across the border. Life was uncertain, especially for many who had moved several times and who usually had no opportunity for education. Most of these citizens took comfort in the Baptist faith with its own explicitness and were much displeased with Mormon ideas about representing Christ's true church, and expecting momentarily to be gathered to Heaven, leaving behind unbelievers.

It troubled many observers also that most Mormons were Yankees who often had some education. Claiming to converse with a God who directed them to be cordial to the Indians, the Mormons wanted to make the red man welcome at the gathering of the faithful. For many skeptics, this view about Indians was alone sufficient to prove the Saints either seditious or insane, or both. Most Jackson County citizens could see nothing saintly in the Indian who was reportedly lurking over the border with murder and pillage on his savage mind. Even more alarming was the Mormon attitude toward the free blacks. Not only were the Saints opposed to bondage, but they were ready to admit the freedman into their circle. In addition to such striking views, the Mormons were clannish, working closely amid themselves and seeming to ignore the needs of the larger community. Their disapproval of whiskey and tobacco also astounded some hardbitten sinners who were members of the first families of western Missouri.

Beginning in 1833 these Saints endured six years of brutality. The war upon the Mormons was intermittent, ranging through such counties as Jackson, Clay, Ray, Caldwell, and Daviess, with the victims occasionally managing to thwart their molesters. The persecution began with one of the great modern meteor showers in November 1833. Many Jackson County citizens took this as a sign that the end predicted by the Mormons was at hand, and they hastened to drive the Saints out of their area. Rarely did the Saints have any peace, although they seemed to prosper wherever they tarried. Most of them were pushed into the prairie countryside of Caldwell County, which a desperate Missouri legislature created in the understanding that it would be a preserve for the Saints. With awesome and dismaying growth, the Mormons spread even into the adjacent Daviess County on the north.

Their endurance did not prevent the Saints from quarreling over tactics. Should force replace moral example? Should they develop a secret police system? These questions were roused by the suffering from years of pillaging and murder. While the prophet, Joseph Smith, wavered on the issues, usually counseling patience until the Lord's time should arrive, not all of his lieutenants were so pacific. On 4 July 1838, Sidney Rigdon, a power among the Saints, made a notorious address to a throng in Far West, a town in Caldwell County which had become the Mormons' capital. Rigdon announced that patience was at an end, and thereafter all foes would move against the Saints at peril of their lives. This speech was reprinted across Missouri, intensifying the alarm about rumors concerning Joseph Smith's new Armies of Israel. After the Mormons found themselves barred from voting, their forces appeared to be moving in a threatening manner during August 1838. Other Missourians quickly responded, out of terror, greed, or bloodthirstiness, so that murder, burning, looting, and whipping became commonplace around Caldwell County.

For a time the worst was probably postponed by the curious fact that the prophet's attorneys, Alexander W. Doniphan and David R. Atchison, each commanded a detachment of militia assigned to keep order. After these two persuaded Smith to refrain from reprisals, the Mormons appealed for general support and restitution to Gov. Lilburn W. Boggs. No aid was forthcoming since Boggs's residence and political base were in Jackson County, where no one dared display sympathy for the Saints. Discouraged, Smith finally accepted the advice of his more militant associates. In October 1838, the prophet announced that since soft answers had not turned away wrath, the Saints would fight. Had not Governor Boggs advised them to take care of themselves?

Brief though it was, Missouri's first civil war then began in earnest. Frustrated Mormons attacked the town of Gallatin, looting and burning in a style matching that of their foes. This and other deeds were signals to the Saints' neighbors and to Jefferson City that the Mormons intended to lay waste northwestern Missouri. On 27 October, Governor Boggs issued orders which the militia had early awaited. Labeling the Saints an outrage upon the name of Missouri, the governor directed that they be driven from the state or exterminated; meanwhile he took the precaution of removing the peaceable David Atchison from any command. Three days later, militiamen gave a terrible indication of how literally the governor's command was followed. Two hundred men fell upon a Mormon hamlet at Haun's Mill and quickly killed seventeen Saints, of whom the lucky ones were shot, the less fortunate hacked to death with corn choppers. Only by fleeing to the woods were some Mormons able to escape; the militia spared not even children, and departed leaving the dead unburied and the wounded begging for help.

When news of the massacre reached the main body of Mormons gathered at Far West with Joseph Smith, they chose to parley with the governor's army encamped outside the town. Amid confusion over the conditions, Smith and other leaders surrendered for what they thought were discussions. Immediately the town of Far West was plundered by the troops, with all Mormons forced to yield their land and property as payment for the trouble they were said to have caused. The militia commander, Maj. Gen. Samuel D. Lucas, gave Smith and his associates a court-martial and ordered their public execution. As it happened, Alexander Doniphan was the officer in charge of the prisoners. He announced that if executions occurred, he would see Lucas prosecuted for murder. Facing an implacable Doniphan, Lucas relented.

With their leaders imprisoned, the Mormons made one last attempt to remain in their chosen land. They appealed in December 1838 to the Missouri General Assembly, recounting their years of injury from mob violence, property expropriation, and now an order by Governor Boggs to leave the state. Requesting restitution, the Saints pleaded to stay in Missouri.

The legislators faced an awkward situation. A significant part of the state was becoming indignant at the horrors in the northwestern counties. However, not only was the dignity of the governor at stake, but the legislators knew that a revelation of the facts would disclose how a member of their own body had participated in the slaughter at Haun's Mill. Consequently, the truth was suppressed and the Saints were told to depart. Led by the rising figure of Brigham Young, most of the 15,000 surviving Mormons left Misssouri for Illinois in February 1839. In April, Joseph Smith apparently had the inspiration to bribe a guard with a jug of Missouri corn whiskey. The prophet and his lieutenants escaped, heading for Nauvoo, Illinois, where Smith would be even less fortunate.

After the slaying of Joseph Smith in 1844, most of the Mormons chose to leave the United States for life near the Great Salt Lake. There were some, however, who clung to the early belief that God's Zion was in Jackson County, Missouri. Many of these faithful also refused to accept the stories about their prophet's supposed indiscretions, including alleged sexual liaisons with a number of his women followers. Rejecting the leadership of Brigham Young, these members gathered around Smith's widow, Emma, and her son. They began returning in 1867 to a Jackson County exhausted and sobered by long years of Civil War. Independence once again became Zion, this time for the Reorganized Church of Jesus Christ of Latter-day Saints. Results from this renewal were quite the reverse of experiences in the 1830s, and the thriving Saints became an invaluable element as western Missouri struggled to rebuild. As for Independence, the old frontier town settled back with the Saints to watch the rise of Zion.

When the Saints returned to Jackson County, the region was trying to forget the devastating anguish which came after 1850. In what should then have been her best years of growth and maturation, Missouri was emaciated by a generation of hatred and fear. The tragedy was the more unspeakable since the objects of such feeling were often other Missourians, and internal conflict brought a long oppression of Missouri's spirit. Harry

Truman's mother, for instance, never forgot the unrelenting terror and wide brutality which began in the 1850s over slavery. The causes of the distress had also entailed repudiating Thomas Hart Benton. David R. Atchison, who had been Benton's senatorial colleague since 1843, differed with Benton almost as much as David Barton had. Now it was Atchison who had Missouri's support, leaving Benton behind. This stunning reversal came from the issue of slavery, once considered forever buried by the Missouri Compromise.

With the discovery of gold in California in 1849, ownership of the Indian country west of Missouri became controversial, for it was evident that the area, to be known as Kansas and Nebraska, needed territorial organization if dependable lines of communication were to stretch between the Mississippi valley and the glittering Pacific Coast. As the future of Kansas was debated, geography and politics began once more to torment Missouri and the nation, for with even Missouri's Atchison championing slavery's migration to Kansas, the Missouri Compromise was in mortal peril. As a slave state, Missouri tended to sympathize when southerners claimed a right to enter new federal land with their bondsmen. Additionally, one of the few areas where slavery actually appeared to thrive in Missouri was along the Kansas border. Counties like Jackson feared that a free state just to the west could tempt slaves to escape. Consequently, much of Missouri approved when the Kansas-Nebraska Bill of 1854 made slavery possible if the settlers of Kansas wished it.

With an apprehensive nation watching, western Missouri began behaving as if determined to have slaves in Kansas at any price. The issue seemed to turn the onetime guardian of peace, David Atchison, into an engineer of violence. Atchison openly began encouraging what he enjoyed calling "border ruffians," those Missourians who rushed into the new Kansas Territory to assure political decisions favoring a slave society. The unusual feature was that after voting in Kansas, these interested parties would immediately return to their Missouri homes. In the first Kansas election in November 1854, more than half the votes were cast by Missourians, although the territorial governor had begged that Kansas be left alone. As a result, a territorial delegate who favored slavery was dispatched to Congress.

When Kansas Territory chose her first legislature in March 1855, nearly 5,000 Missourians, including students from the university, marched into the area to vote with flags, firearms, knives, and whiskey. The American people watched an amazing outcome, which was not that the proslavery side won, but that more than 6,000 votes were cast in a territory boasting barely 2,000 eligible voters. Senator Atchison himself led a large group of these Missourians, who he claimed were acting to assure slavery's safety across to the Pacific Coast and to preserve the principle of unrestricted territories.

The controversy did not stop, however, with the dubious voting practices. Arrival of the New England Emigrant Aid Society and other eastern organizations so outraged many western Missourians that they agreed with Senator Atchison's astounding talk of treating these "Negro heroes" as Mormons. This treatment was known to mean shooting, burning, and hanging, methods doubly senseless since slaveholders were a distinct minority in Missouri. On the western border, however, owners of 50,000 slaves were a significant group, and a threat to them quickly became to many sympathetic neighbors a menace to Missouri generally.

Nevertheless, opposition to slavery appeared to increase in Kansas. David Atchison gave himself entirely to the challenge, scarcely attending to senatorial duties and refusing to stand for re-election in 1856. Yet despite Atchison and the men he summoned to join him with their firearms, the opponents of slavery managed to enter Kansas. Attempts at blocking their passage on the Missouri River were fruitless since most free-soilers entered Kansas from Iowa. Making the town of Lawrence their center, the antislavery forces asserted that the Missouri-inspired government for Kansas was a nullity, inciting a band that included Atchison and other Missourians to raid Lawrence in the spring of 1856. The town was pillaged and three citizens died, so enraging an abolitionist named John Brown who lived nearby in Osawatomie that he quickly struck back, thereby gaining national notoriety. Brown led raiders to a proslave settlement on Pottawatomie Creek, where five of the squatters were murdered.

Nothing less than war between Missouri and Kansas ensued. Atchison brought a retaliatory force of a thousand men to put down Brown and others of like mind while the free-state men organized for defense. Violent encounters resulted until the autumn of 1857 when fresh election returns showed that Kansas had been claimed by free-soil sentiment, despite everything Missouri had done. Then the scene shifted to Missouri as Kansans took their turn in making forays into Missouri, motivated at times by what they only imagined to be threats, and at other times by vengeance. The assailants from Kansas, known as Jayhawkers, included John Brown, who on one occasion carried away eleven slaves after slaying their Missouri owner.

Eventually, the two governors managed to calm the violence until the election of 1860 brought new terrors in the border area, producing horrors that made western Missouri a most melancholy area in this time of greatest torment. Meanwhile, David Atchison returned to private life as a farmer, having helped mightily to make "Bleeding Kansas" a national outcry. He emerged momentarily during the Civil War, but only to seek aid from his old friend, Jefferson Davis, for Missouri's secessionists.

Curiously, at the height of the bloodletting between Missouri and Kansas, the federal Supreme Court chose in 1857 to speak on the disputed question of congressional power over slavery in the territories. At issue was the effort of a Missouri slave from the St. Louis area, Dred Scott, to secure his freedom. Scott's owner had once taken him north into a region presumably closed by the Missouri Compromise. When the Court held that Congress was powerless to exercise such restrictions on property, many persons thought this decision against Dred Scott implied that slavery would be safe anywhere. Missouri's notoriety from this case and from the border brutalities had an ironic feature, however, for while the nation prepared to split over issues heavily involving the state, a spirit of moderation seemed to arise in Missouri.

At no time was Missouri's political caution better exhibited than during the election of 1860 and the months thereafter. Slavery may have been a unifying element in the statehood excitement around 1820, but it was not a compelling force in the minds of most Missourians in 1860. In that year slaves constituted less than 10 percent of the population. Out of Missouri's nearly 1.2 million citizens, fewer than 25,000 were slaveholders. While the Negro bondsman doubtless had an important moral meaning for many citizens, especially the German and Irish laboring community around St. Louis, much of the state entered the war era more concerned about pitfalls along the political paths taken by extremists in both North and South. Most Missourians probably would gladly have watched the war from the sidelines, waiting to study the meaning of its outcome. Instead, the war years entangled Missouri perhaps more thoroughly than any other states except Virginia and Tennessee.

Missouri's outlook took shape between the 1860 elections and the meeting of an extraordinary state convention in February and March 1861. In November 1860, most voting Missourians clearly preferred the cautious posture associated with John Bell's Constitutional Union movement or that of the Douglas Democrats. More than 70 percent of the electorate urged accommodation and compromise as approaches to the national crisis. Abraham Lincoln drew only 10 percent of the voters, with the modest balance going to the pro-Southern Democrats. In August, Claiborne Fox Jackson had been elected governor as a moderate Democrat, but three months later he was beginning to talk of great dangers to the state and of the advantages of secession. Toward that end, Jackson urged that Missourians call a special convention to discuss the state's future. Meanwhile, the retiring governor, Robert M. Stewart, remained closer to the state's mood when he pleaded in a farewell address that Missouri not be frightened or stampeded away from the Union into the calamities of secession.

To the astonishment of Claiborne Jackson, the voters followed Stewart's advice and chose not a single advocate of secession to the special 1861 convention. Of the 140,000 votes cast in selecting delegates, only 30,000 went to secessionists. Most of the state's agricultural and business community saw no future in the Confederacy, and even in the principal slave counties sentiment for the Union prevailed. Most Missouri slaveowners took Lincoln at his word that no threat was intended to those regions where bondage existed. Thus, in sharp contrast to the tradition of furor on the state's western border, at St. Louis the ninety-nine convention delegates retained a Stoic calm. The convention agreed that there was no reason to leave the Union and urged every means to reconcile the nation's sections. Similarly, the delegates opposed the use of force against seceding states, and called for a federal constitutional convention.

In spite of this lofty sentiment at St. Louis, Missouri was dragged into the war. The state remained loyal to the Union, although a few secessionist politicians mounted a government in exile which received skeptical recognition by the Confederacy. Perhaps most Missourians were not enthusiastic about either side, but events and the state's location overcame the Olympian mood of withdrawal displayed at the convention. When hostilities arrived, they did so with intense savagery. More than a thousand battles and skirmishes were fought in Missouri, a number of Civil War conflicts exceeded only in Virginia and Tennessee. Sixty percent of Missouri's eligible men served in the war, with nearly three-fourths of them fighting for the Union. Beyond formal encounters between Federal and Confederate forces was a second kind of conflict, guerrilla action which devastated entire counties and left perhaps 27,000 citizens dead. This evil had the more dreadful and enduring feature for it meant violence between neighbors who had been forced out of desperation to suspect one another of conspiracy and brigandage.

The catastrophe which marked the war's arrival in Missouri illustrated what would be its special tragedy for the state: the Camp Jackson affair in May 1861. Governor Jackson inclined toward the Confederacy, but Frank Blair and certain other St. Louis leaders were determined that the state should remain in the Union. After refusing Lincoln's call for volunteers from Missouri, Jackson ordered the state militia to train for defensive engagements. Meanwhile, Blair was organizing Home Guard units, ostensibly to maintain orderly membership in the Union.

Uneasiness increased when Governor Jackson established a militia training camp, named after himself, on the edge of St.
Louis. Not only did the proximity of troops alarm Unionist leadership in St. Louis, but it also seemed to menace the Federal arsenal nearby. When Unionists learned that President Jefferson
Davis was sending Confederate arms for the governor's militia,
the Home Guard, by then serving as Federal troops under
Gen. Nathaniel Lyon, forced the surrender of Camp Jackson.

A carnage then occurred in St. Louis streets between fellow
Missourians. As some citizens, serving as the governor's militia, were led as prisoners by other citizens, acting as Federal
volunteers, spectators threw rocks and eventually fired a shot.
When a Federal soldier fell dead, the troops were ordered to
defend themselves against what appeared to be a pro-Southern
mob. After the troops fired on the crowd, general disorder ensued until twenty-eight persons were slain and many were
wounded. Thus were Missourians pitched suddenly against each
other in a senseless and confused setting. The episode made it
impossible for moderates to restrain those citizens who wished
to believe Governor Jackson's plea that Missouri must defend
herself against invasion.

Until the St. Louis killings, Jackson had little success in getting the legislature interested in military measures. After Camp
Jackson, the govenor found at least some of the enthusiasm he
needed. One person who came to Jackson's side was Sterling
Price, a former governor who had served splendidly in the Mexican War and who had been chairman of the St. Louis Convention which four months earlier had momentarily kept the state
on lofty ground. Although he accepted command of the state
guard, Price worked at keeping the war from entering Missouri
so that Jefferson Davis was much bewildered, especially when
Price insisted that Confederate troops not slip into Missouri. He
also reached an agreement with the commander of Federal
troops in St. Louis, Gen. William S. Harney, intended to keep
Missouri aloof from the war. However, Unionists such as Frank
Blair and Nathaniel Lyon thwarted this accommodation through
Harney's removal. Then, in a meeting with Governor Jackson
and General Price at the Planter's House, Blair and Lyon an-

nounced that neutrality was impossible, leaving Jackson and Price little choice but to hasten out of St. Louis toward Jefferson City with their troop escort burning bridges as they went.

With the failure of the Planter's House conference all hope of calm in Missouri ended. Calling for Missourians to support Price's state guard, Governor Jackson abandoned the capital, hoping to find a safer spot. On 15 June 1861, General Lyon and his federal volunteers claimed Jefferson City. By late July a new governor and administration sat in the capitol, a reasonable feat since the St. Louis Convention which had placed Missouri close to the Union in March now reconvened and unanimously named Hamilton R. Gamble provisional governor. Vexed by ill-health, this son of Virginia who had come to Missouri in 1818 managed with considerable genius and enormous patience to restore and maintain a moderate spirit in the state. As provisional governor, Gamble pursued President Lincoln's hope that Missouri would stand calmly in the Union. Believing that such a posture required reconciliation, Gamble offered amnesty to penitent followers of Jackson and Price, and created a new state militia whose purpose was to release Federal troops for duty in the East.

Gamble's tactics exemplified cautious Missouri behavior. Especially did he seek to avoid factionalism since Missouri's most wrenching problem involved the dissidents who sought revenge, whether through guerrilla action or agitation over slavery's future. Gamble chose not to make his continuation as governor a matter of electoral dispute, remaining on provisional status. Until his death early in 1864, Gamble gamely struggled for a moderate Missouri while trying to manage wartime affairs despite a rival Missouri government in exile. Probably the least of Gamble's burdens was the rump government which fled first to Arkansas and then to Texas. At an October 1861 meeting while in flight, the remnant general assembly voted to secede from the Union. Within a few months, however, Confederate forces had retreated into Arkansas, and Missouri ceased to be a contested area. In December 1862 Claiborne Jackson died in Arkansas, his cause in Missouri reduced to irregular activities by covert sympathizers. Missouri's exiled administration took part in Southern affairs through representation in the Confederate Congress.

General Sterling Price was far more successful than Claiborne Jackson in vexing the Gamble government. Hailed by his devoted men as "Old Pap," Price had a colorful career during the Civil War, surviving to return to Missouri after Lee's surrender. In 1861 Price struggled valiantly to gain control of the Missouri River. His hopes of freeing the state from federal captivity rose when he defeated Nathaniel Lyon's forces near Springfield at the Battle of Wilson's Creek on 10 August 1861. The Union forces were unable to supply Lyon with reinforcements and Lyon was ordered to avoid the fight. But Lyon fought, lost, and was killed. Price urged that all Missourians rally to his cause, but when few recruits appeared, he was obliged to move south into Arkansas and to eventual defeat at the Battle of Pea Ridge on 7 and 8 March 1862.

Legend about Sterling Price persisted long after the Civil War. Before Pea Ridge he had not lost a battle or a skirmish. For a time thereafter, he served the Confederacy east of the Mississippi, returning in autumn 1864 to attempt a last invasion of Missouri. Accompanied by Gen. Joseph O. Shelby, a colorful Missourian who rode a mule as a Confederate cavalry leader, Price created more alarm than damage as he moved through the state. Entering from the southeast, Price hoped his 12,000 men could take St. Louis and Jefferson City, but his plan was thwarted by his own mistakes at Pilot Knob and by capable Federal action. Finally, in a decisive battle fought in Jackson County at Westport on 23 October 1864, Price recognized he was beaten and hurried south once more to Arkansas. Missouri's great size had compelled him to march his men 1,500 miles in this final foray across the state.

Although Sterling Price and Jo Shelby, among the best of the Confederacy's leadership, had not proved a serious military menace to Missouri, Governor Gamble's leadership was undermined by another facet of the war, the bitterness left by guerrilla action. Distressing though the fighting against the Confederate army was for Missourians, it left memories far different from the shots from a wooded ambush or the raids of bushwhackers.

The pattern of brutality which Missourians along the western border had dreaded in the 1850s reappeared throughout the state after 1861. Many followers of "Old Pap" Price preferred to slip back home, there to continue supporting the Confederate cause by swift assaults on neighbors of different views. These sneak attacks brought retaliation in kind, a pattern guaranteed to make suspicion and hatred flourish.

Governor Gamble, local authorities, and military officials all were driven to desperation by the irregular war. Missouri witnessed the sort of struggle which a century later would unhorse France and then the United States in Southeast Asia. Over a century before the Vietnam War, Missouri had become accustomed to murder, robbery, and pillage against public and private individuals by persons who slipped away unrecognized to reappear the next day as seemingly innocent neighbors. When infuriated citizens played the role of avenging militia, the reprisals were often equally savage and unjust. As the war years passed, great sections of Missouri became desolate. Many families were split in opinion and riven by suspicion. In the face of murder, atrocities, and even confiscation of property, numerous Missourians found themselves rootless as refugees. Their plight depicted how the informal war made the agony of army conflict relatively modest. Nevertheless, Governor Gamble stuck to his much criticized policy of relying upon local authority to keep what order was possible.

Shooting and looting became a way of life for some Missourians. Especially in western areas organized bands tried to use the guise of Robin Hood to prey upon citizens, ostensibly in the cause of an oppressed Confederacy. However, these gangs were matched in abominable behavior by units of Kansans who considered it a duty to enter Missouri on errands of vengeance against such famed outlaw leaders as William Quantrill, "Bloody Bill" Anderson, and Cole Younger. Quantrill, who held a captaincy in the Confederate army, and his men made a specialty of avenging western Missouri after raids by Kansans. Although he by no means confined his murderous ways to Kansas, Quantrill's most infamous excursion was a raid upon Lawrence on 21 August 1863. There his gang undertook to kill every male large enough to carry a gun, slaying 150 men and burning 185 buildings. Ghastly though this was, Quantrill had to share infamy with Bill Anderson and his boys. For instance, the Anderson gang looted the mid-Missouri town of Centralia on 27 September 1864, taking the opportunity to remove twenty-four Federal soldiers from a passing train. These troops, unarmed and on furlough, were murdered and the train burned. To Quantrill and Anderson, any game seemed fair.

Such atrocity, both by notorious gangs and the unknown terrorists, brought pleas, even from powers outside Missouri, for decisive retaliation. Governor Gamble was blamed by some for permitting his concern about reconciliation to outweigh punishing such brutality. After Quantrill's massacre of Lawrence, calls for retribution were especially shrill, with Kansas demanding that the region around Kansas City be subdued, claiming it was the desperadoes' nest. Western Missourians, especially in Jackson, Clay, Bates, Platte, and Cass counties, rejected this demand, arguing that an even worse trail of blood and ruins had been cut through Missouri by the Jayhawkers. A leader among these Kansas gangs was James H. Lane, who believed all Missourians to be evil slave masters. When Lane was not creating havoc in Missouri, he was serving as United States senator from Kansas. Eventually, pressure from Kansas forced the commander of the military district around Kansas City, Maj. Gen. Thomas Ewing, to act.

No policy adopted by either the Federal or Southern armies was more controversial than Ewing's General Order No. 11, dated 25 August 1863. It decreed that all farm dwellers in the border counties of Jackson, Bates, Cass, and in part of Vernon County, were to abandon their homes and property within a fortnight. Exception was made for families living near a Federal military post. There, persons of proven loyalty could take refuge. All others were to leave the district—which in Ewing's suspicious mind meant virtually everyone in the area. Such an order appeared inordinately cruel and excessive. To worsen matters, Ewing's sympathy with Kansas extremists led him to summon Kansas cavalry men to help enforce the order, which added to Missouri's humiliation.

Leading the Kansas troops was Charles R. "Doc" Jennison, who rivaled Lane and Quantrill as a villainous leader of gang action. Jennison and his men went to work with zeal, making the Missouri border counties a burned wasteland. Thousands of Missourians fled to eastern counties leaving their possessions to the elated Kansans. For the latter, it was an exercise of justice in behalf of the widows and orphans created by Quantrill's destruction of Lawrence. General Ewing took satisfaction in the action, believing it eliminated the supply base for the Missouri gangs, forcing the latter to scatter. However, such methods made Ewing notorious, thanks especially to the outrage of George Caleb Bingham, who used the incident for one of his most celebrated paintings. As one of Ewing's staff members, Bingham had pleaded against the policy, warning of the consequences. Bingham's "Order No. 11" became one of America's most famous historical paintings, requiring only a glance to see the artist's success in displaying Missouri's torment. A desperate Ewing was left to mutter that Bingham did not understand war.

When the war was over Southern sympathizers, especially, tended to make men like Quantrill and Anderson legendary heroes. The brutality used to subdue the gangs converted the ruffians' own ghastly practices into acts of defense and noble revenge. The continuing lawlessness after 1865 involved many men like Jesse James who had previously plundered the countryside, either for the South or the North. Their raids upon an unpopular postwar government and society in turn burnished the memory of the wartime bushwhackers. The attacks of these thieving gangs as well as stories of the wantonness during the war were translated by numerous Missourians into courageous repudiations of malevolent or wrongheaded government.

Governor Gamble had tried to spare Missouri this inheritance of division and punishment. By the time Gamble died, early in 1864, such hope was doomed. Instead of a state where the brotherhood of Missourians prevailed over the clamor of battle in the East, internecine warfare and political hatred were in command. After Gamble's death, Missouri was gripped by a political aspect of the inner torment which centered upon two important issues—how to handle the emancipation of slaves and how to place postwar Missouri in the right hands. Resolution of these problems usually meant that power went to those who had been ardent Unionists, thereby destroying the old Democratic party. These issues produced two state constitutions and four remarkable leaders. Each of these men, Frank Blair, B. Gratz Brown, Charles Drake, and Carl Schurz served Missouri in the United States Senate and attained national distinction. Two of them were nominees for vice-president, Blair in 1868 and Brown in 1872. All were profoundly interested in how Missouri, still one of America's most important states, would return to national leadership.

Blair, Brown, and Schurz wanted to recreate Missouri through tolerance, but Charles Drake evidently believed that revenge upon the disloyal citizens was most important. Drake and others united early to challenge Gov. Hamilton Gamble's moderation. They were especially impatient with talk of ending slavery gradually, preferring immediate freedom. Furthermore, they wanted to avoid making it easy for rebels to regain full citizenship. Charles Drake was an enigmatic figure. Before the war he was hardly distinguished, known as a capable speaker who seemed to favor slavery. However, by 1863 Drake had changed his views. Seizing upon the fearfulness and anger brought by the war, he produced a political radicalism which served to deepen Missouri's torment although he talked of a new, forward-looking state. So skillfully did Drake play upon the strained emotions of many loyal and embittered Missourians that it was difficult even for courageous men to oppose him.

Drake and his associates refused to accept the moderate program Missouri established in 1863 which would free the slaves on 4 July 1870 but leave slaves past forty years of age as servants permanently indentured to their former owners. Nor could Drake condone the test oaths which the Gamble government used to prevent secessionist sympathizers from influencing the electoral and legislative processes. While these oaths certainly aimed to sideline persons who had taken up arms against the Union or assisted in the rebellion, they had a gentle spirit about them. For Drake's growing legion of followers, the circumstances did not call for restraint. They believed that past evils demanded a rigorous new righteousness. Drake saw himself leading Missouri's struggle for good against evil. Just as he had once championed laws to preserve the Sabbath, now Drake sought to purify Missouri.

The principal step was to rewrite Missouri's constitution. So dominant was Drake at the St. Louis convention of 1865 that the resultant document was known thereafter as "Drake's constitution." As the convention met, news of enlarged guerrilla and gang violence in Missouri as well as Lincoln's assassination seemed proof to the wavering that Drake was correct in demanding completely loyal men and the subjugation of all others. The convention thus became the high-water mark of hatred and fear in Missouri's public affairs. With a young and inexperienced membership, the meeting proceeded first to exercise what it claimed as the right to enact ordinances. On 11 January 1865, it voted immediate freedom to all slaves, thereby making Missouri the first slave state to put an end to black bondage. However, the convention's ideas about a pure Missouri prohibited the newly freed blacks from voting and holding office.

In fact, the question of which Missourians might safely be entrusted with office was, next to emancipation, the convention's main concern. Fearful that its good works might be undone by unsympathetic incumbents, the convention voted a famous "Ousting Ordinance" which declared vacant on 1 May 1865 the positions of all judges, county clerks, circuit attorneys, sheriffs, and county recorders. Unfinished terms would be completed by new men appointed by the governor, a Drake associate. When this action, which dislodged some 800 officials, was opposed by the Missouri Supreme Court, the Drake Radicals had members of that bench forcibly removed.

Controversial as this measure was, it was mild compared to the scheme placed in the new constitution to assure that all public offices, church pulpits, and various professions would be occupied only by those whom Missouri's new conscience deemed fit. This device, known as the "Ironclad Oath," carried into peacetime Missouri much of the war's tormented spirit. Drake himself evidently wrote the second section of the constitution which ordered prospective voters, officeholders, clergy-men, teachers, jurors, and attorneys to swear innocence to numerous acts considered disloyal. Eighty-six such deeds were listed as a basis for denying the right of franchise. The state was organized into voting districts as a means for efficiently administering the oath.

Many nominally loyal citizens were appalled at the prospect of banishing so many Missourians from state affairs. Even Gov. Thomas C. Fletcher at first opposed the constitution. Edward Bates, whom Lincoln had summoned from Missouri to be attorney general, repudiated the constitution, as did much of the German population, some of whom sensed the rise in Missouri of the illiberality they thought had been left in Europe. So intense was the furor over the oath that little notice was taken of the constitution's attempt to limit the power of the general assembly, to provide public financing for education, and to make business and industry feel more welcome in Missouri.

Drake did everything possible to secure approval of his constitution. The oath for voters was applied even though such a proscription was the subject of the election. Despite this frantic winnowing, Missourians rejected the proposed constitution by nearly a thousand votes. Drake, however, had remembered one possibility and thereby saved his work. He arranged that absent soldiers would vote, and their ballots gave the constitution a victory of less than 2,000 votes. After the constitution's narrow adoption, the state seemed to recoil from what had been done, allowing brilliant opposition to the spirit and letter of the document to begin. Drake's harsh views lost ground quickly, so that even he recognized his plans for a new and purified Missouri were fruitless, prompting him to resign his United States Senate seat for the security of appointment by President Grant as chief justice of the United States Court of Claims.

The United States Supreme Court assisted the assault on Missouri's radicalism by declaring the loyalty oath unconstitutional in restraining persons from professional pursuits. However, the end of Drake's "Reign of Terror" was hastened largely by the opposition of such men as Frank Blair, Carl Schurz, and B. Gratz Brown. Through these three figures, a fusion of Liberal Republicans and Democrats captured a brief enthusiasm for reform, first in Missouri and then nationally. Espousing varied partisan positions, these individuals expressed the widening disgust with Drake's views. They composed a so-called liberal opposition determined to end Missouri's persisting torment by restoring many of the state's old values. Blair, Brown, and Schurz were, of course, only three of numerous individuals drawn into Missouri's political turmoil after 1865 when the moment and the issues seemed unusually compelling. Both Drake's cause and that of the liberal rejoinder had moral urgencies which were appealing at a time when many citizens believed Missouri and the Republic were being reborn.

Of the three leaders in restoration, Blair, Brown, and Schurz, only Frank Blair was so appalled at the vengeful, elitist mood among Republicans that he openly returned to the Democratic fold. Brown and Schurz remained outside in a halfway house of dissent, known as Liberal Republicanism. Before the war, Blair had bolted to the new Republican movement over the free-soil issue. Yet by 1868 Blair's reunion with the Democrats was so complete that he was nominated for vice-president. He had rejoined the Democrats in part because of family and Missouri tradition and, also, because he strongly deplored the cruelties practiced by Charles Drake and other Radicals. In the 1868 campaign Blair traveled in Missouri and across the United States, preaching a simple Jacksonian solution to the torment in the state and nation. His message was a rather vague refrain about letting the people rule, although by this he clearly did not include blacks, since Blair did not support granting any rights to Negroes. In fact, Blair was one of the last prominent Americans to advocate transferring Negroes to some distant colony. When he lost the election, Blair returned to Missouri determined that Drake's policies must somehow be repelled. This effort quickly resulted in a coalition of Blair's tattered Democrats and the Republican dissenters.

A cousin of Frank Blair, B. Gratz Brown, emerged as leader of those Republicans who rejected Drake's program of hate and revenge. Brown was far more generous than his cousin, for he stoutly defended the right to vote not only of blacks but also of women. As a former Benton man, Brown had far less difficulty collaborating with Democrats than did his companion, Carl Schurz, a newly arrived St. Louis journalist who distrusted Blair. Brown and Schurz had broken with the Grant wing of the Republican party for reasons which included more than oppression of Southern sympathizers. In attempting to rally moderate Republicans in Missouri, Brown and Schurz handled issues in a way which appealed to Democrats. They condemned tariffs to protect industry and they urged the cleansing of government through a reform of the civil service. Brown and Schurz were like most Missouri Democrats in rediscovering in postwar conditions such old foes as big government and big business.

Recognizing that a waiting game might allow the state to forgive and forget the secessionist policies of Claiborne Jackson, the Democrats shrewdly played 'possum. For a time after 1865, they stood on the sidelines to cheer Liberal Republicans rather than offering their own candidates. In this way, Gratz Brown was elected governor in 1870, the only Liberal Republican to have that distinction. However, two-thirds of those voting for Brown were Democrats. In contests for the general assembly, old Jacksonians were less timid. Majorities in both houses enabled them to send Frank Blair to the Senate in 1871. Governor Brown's alliance with his prewar Democratic colleagues seemed increasingly natural, as was his use of Jeffersonian phrases in his inaugural address. The new governor urged Missourians to believe that, fundamentally, all were Republicans, all were Democrats.

Brown recognized that most Missourians had cautiously held back from the vindictiveness of Drake's Radicals. Anticipating that the old Missouri was still alive and vital, Brown put away that part of his own past which included near-abolitionist talk and strenuous opposition to secession. Under his leadership the signs of hatred in Missouri receded. Since the state had clung to the Union at fearful cost, Missouri's postwar political discourse was observed by America with particular interest. As Brown and others sought to bring their state out of physical and emotional ruins, their efforts stood out from those of others in the nation struggling over how best to restore desirable values and institutions.

The Liberal Republican movement lasted long enough to bring Missouri a glorious moment. Unity between the dissenting Republicans and Democrats seemed by 1870 to be an exciting success in Missouri. A hint of collaboration had sent Carl Schurz to the federal Senate in 1869, while more co-operation managed to repeal in 1870 the "Ironclad Oath," thereby calmly restoring the vote to 75,000 disfranchised Missourians. The Missouri partnership of Democrats and Liberal Republicans also joined in open revulsion at the odor of corruption from Grant's administration. In general, therefore, many Americans paused to listen as Missouri warned that the spirit of revenge in the nation disguised how old threats to Jefferson's Republic were gaining strength.

Wide attention was given to the call which went out to the nation from a rally of Missouri's Liberal Republicans meeting in Jefferson City in January 1872. Guided by Senator Schurz and Governor Brown, the Missourians urged all Republicans weary of Grantism and Radicalism to convene in Cincinnati on 1 May 1872. It was quietly understood that should these Liberals nominate a presidential candidate, the nation's Democrats would support the ticket. This possibility was largely a result of the collaboration of two Missouri cousins, Governor Brown and Sen. Frank Blair. The latter was spreading the word that only by fusion with the dissenting Republicans could Democrats hope to see the Grant Republicans defeated.

The plan might have come closer to success if the Missouri Liberals had remained united. Governor Brown anticipated being the presidential nominee of the Cincinnati convention until his colleague, Carl Schurz, deserted him to support Charles Francis Adams of Massachusetts. To his Missouri associates Schurz appeared to be motivated by envy. Actually, Schurz, who lacked Gratz Brown's long prewar membership in the Democratic family, was never comfortable as Brown led the Liberal Republicans into closer alliance with the Democrats. Schurz's distrust and dislike for his senatorial colleague, Blair, did nothing to soothe his uneasiness. Consequently, with Missouri suddenly in disarray at the last moment, the Liberal movement stumbled badly and nominated Horace Greeley. Gratz Brown was handed the luckless task of running for vice-president with the controversial and erratic New York editor.

The Democrats dutifully complied with the tacit understanding contained in the Missouri plan, and themselves nominated Greeley and Brown. Although Missouri loyally gave her electoral votes to this team, the larger significance of the 1872 election was evidence that the age of torment was closing. The anti-Radical alliance chose a Democrat, Silas Woodson, to succeed Brown as governor. Woodson's administration immediately proceeded to act in behalf of two of Missouri's old favorites, lower taxes and Spartan government. By 1875 Blair and Schurz had been replaced in the Senate by more traditional Democrats. Schurz himself had bitterly predicted that his reward for aiding reconciliation would be to see a Confederate general succeed him. It was Francis M. Cockrell, a brigadier general with the secessionist army, who began a thirty-year career in the Senate by taking Schurz's seat.

Missouri's performance as a leader for national regeneration quietly ended. Gratz Brown officially returned to the Democratic party. Carl Schurz never really came back to Missouri, staying instead in Washington to vex many of his reform-minded associates by taking a cabinet post amid a regular Republican administration. Frank Blair died in 1875, an emotional and physical wreck. Although he may have disappointed himself and his family by his failure to reach the White House, Blair had been of extraordinary service in helping rescue Missouri from the mongers of hate. He was not exactly forgotten: the two statues of Missourians in the federal Capitol's Hall of Fame are of Blair and his mentor, Thomas Hart Benton.

Evidence that the old Missouri caution had regained command was best displayed in 1874 when a near-majority of voters agreed with Governor Woodson that a proposal to write a new constitution was unwise. Woodson did not for a moment deny that the Drake constitution should be replaced, but he argued that the need was not great enough to merit the high financial cost of a convention. However, a constitutional convention did receive a scant summons and met during the summer of 1875 to produce the instrument by which Missouri was governed for the next seventy years. The work was done by a body in which more members had served for the Confederacy than for the Union and whose chairman, Waldo P. Johnson, had fought under Sterling Price and had represented Missouri in the Confederate Senate. Earlier he had briefly been one of Missouri's members of the United States Senate. The resultant constitution, which was overwhelmingly approved by an unexcited electorate, displayed a distrust of government that might have dismayed even Thomas Jefferson. Among other things, it drastically curbed any potential tendency by the state to be profligate in matters of taxes, debt, and lending. The constitution eventually became so serious a handicap in a changing economy that its limits on public indebtedness and tax rates had to be circumvented openly.

In 1875, however, Missouri appeared to look forward to peaceful days when the old caution and simplicity could once more assert themselves. The end of torment was demonstrated by the visit Jefferson Davis made to Missouri in 1875. The former president of the Confederacy marched across the state to applause, stopping in Fulton for an especially emotional moment in the "Kingdom of Callaway County," a title earned when the neighborhood had been Missouri's stoutest defender of the Southern cause. Curously, St. Louis was host on the same day to President Grant and Jefferson Davis. The two old foes did not meet in what would surely have been a spectacular demonstration of Missouri's triumphant reconciliation. However, for most Missourians the restoration of the Democratic party and the creation of a new constitution expressing a deeply cautious spirit were evidence enough that Missouri's long season of trouble was ending.

8

Jeffersonian Missouri: Truman's Era

N closing the long years of torment and disorder, Missouri sought the assurance and peaceableness which most citizens associated with the Jeffersonian world of small farms and modest business. This Arcadian dream had made Missouri a stalwart Democrat before the Civil War and it spurred her return to that party after 1872. Actually, Missouri's basic values were not far from those of the Confederacy: both praised limited government and rural supremacy. Alas, however, the road back to such benign circumstance was barred by economic and social forces which were already transforming America. Missouri felt so abandoned by the rush toward industrialism that at times she even doubted the fidelity of the Democratic party. The state's occasional flirtations with the Republicans after 1900 were actually only moments when she was pouting over what she fancied as Democratic faithlessness to the precepts of Jeffersonian society. In 1972, for instance, Missouri supported Richard Nixon for president mostly because his modern qualities were less appalling to her than those of his Democratic rival, George McGovern.

Missouri's stubborn insistence upon the continued vitality of old maxims about limited government and simple society has often cast her as a conservative laggard if not as a bitter obstructionist. National trends kept Missouri so alarmed after 1880 that young men like Harry S. Truman grew up in an atmosphere of embattled principles. Truman's was to be the second voice from Missouri demanding that the nation maintain the orthodoxy of the Republic's Jeffersonian founders. Thomas Hart Benton and Harry Truman were linked by a tradition of watchfulness against ancient threats, a wariness shared by many Missourians. While neither Truman nor Benton was comfortable with abstractions, each reiterated the old Missouri displeasure with privilege, taxes, banks, eastern values, and faceless politics. Each also displayed a stubborn—some would call it mule-like—conviction which gave their defense of Missouri values a pugnacity befitting those claiming that free men were always surrounded by enemies calling for battle.

During Truman's youth Missouri was most often represented by men noted for negativism or self-serving colorfulness. In large part this outlook stemmed from the state's remarkable experiences amid the reform enthusiasm of the late nineteenth and early twentieth centuries. Missouri briefly joined this crusade, assuming that the struggle was at heart an effort to undo change and to bring the nation back from the temptations of industrial and finance capitalism. Coming largely from rural areas, most of Missouri's leaders were distressed because many counties were hopelessly in debt for having yielded to the prospect of railroad miracles. Both local indebtedness and agricultural depression strengthened Missouri's fears for rural dignity.

Appropriately, therefore, the National Grange or Patrons of Husbandry had its finest numerical success in Missouri. In 1875, the Grange's best year, Missouri reported more than 2,000 local Grange units. To Missourians, the Grange's emphasis on a dignified and rational agricultural civilization promised to restore the state on the foundations laid by Jackson and Jefferson. Besides education and fraternization in behalf of better husbandry, the Grange fostered unity against the menace of bankers, railroad agents, and industrialists. So put upon by these forces did many Missourians feel during the economic slump which began in 1873 that they founded a short-lived People's party in 1874.

This movement claimed that Missouri's needs were very simple. The members, mostly farmers, wanted lawlessness ended, railroads regulated, rivers and streams improved, public education strengthened, national tariff levels lowered, and state government simplified. Finally, the People's movement adopted the commandment so fundamental in Missouri which said that all proper public ends could be attained while taxes were significantly reduced. No matter how desperate they were, Missouri agrarians did not step out of character. A deepened caution about public policy reinforced in Missouri the idea that dangerous change was much less likely if government had very little money to spend. Beginning with the 1874 People's movement, Missourians made a specialty of demanding that government be a more effective monitor of evils, but with a decreasing revenue.

With the People's movement in 1874 and thereafter in the Democratic party, a rural-based caution took even stronger command of the state's political viewpoint. Since Democratic success in Missouri increasingly required binding the bootheel and Little Dixie agriculturalists with the city machines, no other state more vividly displayed the tragicomic plight of American political parties. Missouri's Democrats had to be ingenious to keep conflicting interests together for the presidential vote. On the other hand, controlling the governor's office rarely caused much excitement. Since Gratz Brown's time, that position was not often filled by a dynamic figure, able or inclined to rally the divided and conservative general assembly. The assembly remained a strained confederation from the state's diverse interests, so that Missouri government often depended upon an understanding between weak governors and recalcitrant legislatures, both relying on the familiar Jeffersonian cautions and suspicions.

Occasional splits in Missouri's political arrangements meant division between two conservative positions. An example can be seen in the career of David R. Francis, who, after serving as St. Louis mayor, became one of Missouri's ablest governors in 1889. As a prudent Democratic administrator, Francis managed to lower taxes while reducing the state's debt. He also championed such causes as the Australian ballot; legislation outlawing railroad pools, trusts, and combinations; an efficient means of choosing public school textbooks; and new strength for the

University of Missouri after a disastrous fire on the campus in 1892. However, Francis refused to follow many fellow Democrats into the silver coinage movement, an action that gave Missouri differing voices from her major party, each claiming greater loyalty to the state's cherished values. Francis insisted that the reliability of the gold standard was more soundly in the state's tradition whereas the rural inflationists thought a flood of silver coins would somehow be safe.

Governor Francis's administration proved Missouri willing to endure a number of the early progressive statutes. These were mostly cautionary enactments, however, carrying a defensive flavor dear to the Missouri suspicion of energetic government or business. Francis's tactics were shared by several other Missouri statesmen whose spirit was less progressive than restorative in tone. Richard Bland, Joseph W. Folk, and Champ Clark, like David Francis, were predecessors of Harry Truman as Missourians who wanted to see their neighbors and the nation once again on the straight and narrow path of Jeffersonian virtue. While Missouri was hardly the only state to enjoy using progressive slogans to march toward the past, she did so with an alacrity which did proud justice to the tradition of Benton. In fact, Richard P. Bland, who was twelve times elected by Missourians to Congress, made a bid for the presidency by rekindling the old concern over the character of money. As with Benton's title of "Old Bullion," Bland received his nickname, "Silver Dick," because he insisted upon coining money, but his goal was quite apart from Benton's.

Bland was aided by the discovery of great quantities of silver in the American West which, if coined, would increase the money in circulation. Enemies argued that Bland actually advocated debasing the money supply when he talked of the unlimited coinage of silver. They said free silver would produce the same evil results which bank notes had brought to Benton's time. However, most Missourians were ready to believe Bland since he cast the problem in familiar terms of an eastern plutocracy persecuting the West by eliminating its silver from the federal monetary system. That view provided a hospitable setting when the proponents of silver coinage gathered in St. Louis in

1889. Delegates from twenty-eight states sought ways to persuade farmers and workers that they were being plundered by a conspiracy, this one made of gold. Bland himself hoped this theme would win him the presidential nomination at the Democratic convention in 1896. However, he was an uninspiring figure who could not dominate the crowds as did William Jennings Bryan with a new face and thrilling voice.

By 1904, the nation's attention had moved beyond the issue of money to questions of greater complexity. Missouri's startling contribution was to insist, in effect, that public affairs were actually little different than at the time of her statehood. Joseph W. Folk used this outlook to take brief command of Missouri's Democratic party, bringing national attention for what was hailed as the "Missouri Idea" which, in essence, stated that the only thing required for the well-being of state and nation was that honest leaders fearlessly enforce simple laws. Folk's was a fleeting episode, built upon one young man's momentary appeal. However, Folk and his "Missouri Idea" displayed succinctly how the state was still dedicated to restoring old values and methods. As a young lawyer from Tennessee, Folk moved to St. Louis to make a career. Soon he was presiding over meetings of alarmed Democrats, appropriately called the Jefferson Club. To this group, economic depression in the 1890s appeared less a problem than the corruption engulfing the city. In this likely setting, Folk developed the "Missouri Idea."

As circuit attorney, Folk succeeded by 1903 in revealing how the government of St. Louis had, under boss Edward Butler, fallen into venality. Folk insisted the problem was elementary, nothing more than that men had betrayed their virtue, the law, and the public. The iniquities disclosed by Folk aroused the ire of most Missourians who, by nature, suspected cities. They thought they recognized another story of votes bought while the tax load was heaped largely on small homeowners and nearby farmers. Folk made the solution to this evil seem simple. He suggested that his state—and America—accept a "Missouri Idea," which was that men had only to insist upon honesty in the process of government. Honesty would always win over privilege and wealth, preached Folk in perfect Jeffersonian orthodoxy. No new legislation nor additional agencies presumably would be needed.

Folk's simple dictum won him the governor's office in 1904, after which he thought of moving to the White House in 1912. In stumping Missouri before his 1904 victory, Folk relentlessly stressed his sublimely appealing version of the old texts. Missouri, he insisted, was on trial before the world, for she must show that democracy could cleanse itself of all corruption by putting down privilege and upholding the law. Folk rarely mentioned other difficulties which afflicted a decaying state. When Folk implied he was the only honest Democrat, many voters evidently believed him, producing such a clamor against the reputed sinfulness of the party that "Holy Joe" Folk himself hastened to concede that not all Democrats were necessarily in need of purification. However, proof of vast corruption in St. Louis and in the general assembly, along with the catcalls and ridicule that traditional Democratic leaders heaped on Folk, were enough to persuade many voters that the time had come to cleanse the party. Folk was the only Democrat chosen in 1904, and Missouri instructed her presidential electors to vote for Theodore Roosevelt, the Republican national candidate, a switch which astounded the nation.

As governor, Folk continued his plea that purity was more important than new legislation. It was enough, he insisted, to enforce the laws on the books. At once he proceeded to aggravate some of his supporters by upholding statutes banning the operation of saloons and dog races on Sunday. Eventually, he did urge some forward-looking legislation concerning corporation responsibilities, child labor distress, and the improvement of roads. As an individual, however, Folk had neither charm nor capacity for political alliance, so that his program drew little enthusiasm in Jefferson City. Disgruntled Democrats were still reminding all who would listen of their faithful stewardship before Joe Folk intruded. Had not the state under his predecessor, Gov. Alexander M. Dockery, paid off the last state bonds? Dockery boasted that Missouri's tax rate had become the lowest in the land. Party regulars considered this real proof of fidelity to the Jeffersonian faith.

Even with a slight Democratic majority in the general assembly after 1906, Folk had little significant success. His unpopularity grew as public disenchantment developed over talk of easy improvement in public affairs. In 1908 he failed to be nominated for the United States Senate and after that he rapidly slipped from public life, although he sought for a time to gain a national reputation through lecture tours. Apparently Joe Folk never discovered what successful battlers for truisms such as Truman and Benton had recognized, that the power of an idea should be harnessed to an organization. Only briefly, therefore, was Folk able to serve the tradition of conservative sloganeering in Missouri. He arrived at a perfect time to challenge the state's uneasiness with political corruption. However, adept largely at antagonizing those whose help he needed for more than slogans, a lonely Folk was able merely to show how readily Missouri responded to calls for restoring the old Republic. He had to yield Missouri's hopes for national attention to Congressman James Beauchamp Clark, whom America came to know as Champ.

Having risen to Speaker of the federal House of Representatives in 1911, Clark's chances seemed excellent to be nominated for president in 1912 by the Democrats. Earlier he had labored loyally for Bryan. He was a highly successful orator, but mostly before rural audiences. As minority leader in the House, he had helped the rebel Republicans change the rules to reduce the power of the Speaker. With this record the 1912 Baltimore Democratic convention on the ninth ballot gave Clark a majority of the delegates, but not the two-thirds margin required. William Jennings Bryan was greatly alarmed by the New York delegation's support of Clark. Bryan abandoned his friend Clark for Woodrow Wilson, and the Missourian saw the presidency slip away because of a supposed bargain with the Robber Barons of Wall Street.

Actually, Clark's major weakness had been the determination of eastern party bosses to nominate Wilson, the governor of New Jersey. Wilson won on the forty-sixth ballot, despite the appeal of an Ozark ballad Clark had made popular. This song expressed the outrage of agriculturalists at the abuse they re-

ceived from city folk. The verses dealt with a Missouri hound
named Jim, making him for a time the most famous dog in
America. The ballad's refrain warned:

> Every time I come to town
> The boys keep kickin' my dawg aroun'
> Makes no dif'erence if he is a houn'
> They gotta quit kickin' my dawg aroun'.

While Champ Clark and the Missouri hound were out search-
ing for the presidency, at home in Missouri there were startling
developments. A Republican had been elected governor in
1908. Embittered by Joseph Folk's manner and accusations,
many Democrats had found Herbert S. Hadley an agreeable
choice. Even though a Republican, he had a reassuring record
as a Kansas City prosecuting attorney who fought urban evils.
After 1904 Hadley was Missouri's attorney general and became
a sensation, battling what he claimed were the trusts and mo-
nopolies threatening the state. Many old Democrats doubtless
reasoned that "Old Bullion" Benton would have applauded
Hadley. As it turned out, however, Governor Hadley and his
Democratic successor, Elliot W. Major, between 1909 and 1917
founded modern Missouri government. In doing so, they
brought Missouri closer to assumption of the burdens of twentieth-century society than the state proved willing to accept.

These two governors believed that the spirit for change then
abroad in America ought to carry Missouri beyond the stale
Jacksonian anger against lawbreakers and economic pirates.
Hadley and Major argued that the state should face enlarged responsibility in such areas as health, environment, transportation,
education, and penal conditions. As a result there were widely
gratifying advances in agricultural extension service, protection
for fish and wildlife, safeguards for waterways, strengthened
supervision of public service corporations and utilities, state
highway management, and child welfare legislation. Where
Hadley and Major failed was in convincing the public that as
more services and human safeguards were provided to Missourians, taxes must rise. When each governor reminded the
general assembly that the cost of the modest progress achieved

was only the beginning of what would be required from the state's revenues, he found Missouri's progressivism cooled rapidly.

Governor Hadley became especially blunt after failure of his efforts to have real and personal property assessed at actual value for tax purposes. He admonished the general assembly that if the people of Missouri were to succeed in enlarging government functions, they would need financial support unanticipated when the constitution was rewritten in 1875. At the close of his term a disappointed Hadley told Missouri that while economy in governance was surely important, the issue should not be how little money might be spent but what expenditures were needed for Missouri's government to have the greatest possible meaning for the people.

Eventually the tax system was modified but in a rising spirit of suspicion and bitterness. Frederick D. Gardner, a Democrat who succeeded Elliot Major as governor in 1917, quickly perceived that most Missourians were outraged at what the state's excursion into progressivism was costing. Alarm was particularly high at the news that the state was in debt and openly practicing deficit spending. While there was no significant effort to undo what Hadley and Major had helped achieve, the public mood was to pay as little as possible and watch suspiciously how the innovations worked. Under Governor Gardner, Missouri adopted modest taxes on incomes, inheritances, and corporate franchises, with a tax commission established to rationalize the property excise. However, beyond this timid attempt to meet the obligations incurred by the progressive legislation most citizens clearly were loath to go. Caught in this revival of Missouri traditionalism, Gardner promised an old-fashioned Jeffersonian administration. When the general assembly approved pensions for the blind and a home for neglected children, Gardner vetoed even these appealing steps on the sound Missouri premise that funds had not been provided for them.

Although proponents of progress, such as Hadley, Folk, and Major, had been mildly successful during the Progressive era, Missouri was happiest when she felt that public affairs would require fewer taxes while all the traditional enemies were being

kept on the run. The momentum begun by Folk and Hadley, un-
typical governors in Missouri's history, brought Missouri only
to the edge of America's new civilization. When most Missourians listened to Woodrow Wilson, they preferred to believe
that his New Freedom policies were aimed at restoring affairs to
an earlier state of decency. Wilson's apostrophes to the age of
Jefferson were probably taken more literally in Missouri than
the champion of a New Freedom may have intended.

Careers of Missourians in the United States Senate displayed
something of Missouri's discomfort in the march of America
Francis M. Cockrell and George G. Vest retained popularity in
Missouri by condemning imperialism. Vest was especially conspicuous as leader of the Senate opposition to annexing the Phil-
ippine Islands. Presently, William J. Stone grew famous for de-
nouncing President Wilson's tendency to become involved in
World War I. As chairman of the Senate Committee on
Foreign Relations, Stone led eleven other senators against the
president's request to arm America's merchant fleet. Despite
Wilson's bitter invectives, Stone implored the nation to resist
war. Even more consistent with Missouri's traditional stance
was Stone's claim, not lost upon many of Missouri's rural and
village citizens, that the drift of national policy had the effect of
giving one man the power to make war.

In April 1917, Stone was one of the six senators to vote
against Wilson's request for resolutions of war, while across in
the House of Representatives, four of Missouri's members also
voted against going to war. Stone made it clear that he considered war the most dreaded exercise of political power, surely as
solemn a Jeffersonian thesis as could be recalled. War's portents
were unpredictable, Stone pointedly observed, as he watched
hysteria develop even in parts of normally skeptical Missouri.
Joined by Champ Clark in the House and James A. Reed in the
Senate, Stone even raised doubts about military conscription
which had to await the Vietnam War to be taken seriously.
However, when World War I actually began, Stone put aside
his opposition. He died in 1918.

For another decade, Stone's companion, James Reed, who
had entered the Senate in 1911, took Missouri's spirit to yet

more spectacular lengths. Not even Stone had been able to agree with Reed's attempt to prevent the government from banning alcoholic beverages. Reed's assault on Prohibition was mild, however, when placed beside his battle to block America's entering the League of Nations, or beside his later denunciations of New Deal policies. Still, Reed's views and personal style made him one of Missouri's most successful, if controversial, Jeffersonians. His career began in 1898 and lasted well beyond his voluntary departure from the Senate in 1929.

As had so many other Missouri politicians, Reed used his oratorical prowess first as a prosecuting attorney, in this case in Jackson County. Thereafter, he was mayor of Kansas City at a time when it was well to speak kindly of reform. However, Reed never approached being a Progressive, for even as late as the 1940s, he opposed the selection of judges on a nonpartisan basis, arguing that the idea was an absurd fraud. Decades earlier, he fought giving the vote to women, on grounds equally candid, again exhibiting the typical Missouri disillusionment with human nature. Perhaps this realistic spirit enabled Reed to speak skillfully on such moving topics as motherhood and freedom while retaining the admiration of his close associate, Tom Pendergast.

Reed's determination to spare America the insidious encroachments of government led him to try for the presidential nomination in 1928 and 1932. Although these futile attempts proved to be painful for Reed's many fellow Missourians who rejoiced in his fight against the old enemies, Senator Reed had earlier enjoyed one memorable victory. In 1922 he won re-election against the kind of odds which his young cohort in Jackson County, Harry Truman, faced on a wider basis in 1948. Reed's opposition to Prohibition, his denunciation of the League of Nations, and his scorn for woman suffrage had led the Democratic leaders to consider him a liability. With "Rid us of Reed" clubs appearing in the state, the unintimidated candidate took his message to hamlets and countryside by camping in a large tent. Reed's skepticism about reform and his shouts against the messianic Woodrow Wilson may have been as useful as was his support from the "wets" and from the political machines in St. Louis and Kansas City.

Reed won handsomely in 1922, a time when even Missouri was tempted to elect Republicans, yet he soon found how difficult life had become for the old Jeffersonian mood. After 1929 he grew increasingly shrill and negative, qualities which seemed to some observers as the only outcome when old ideas stayed too long. Nevertheless, Reed's expression of Missouri misgiving was carried on by Bennett Champ Clark, son of Champ Clark. As Harry Truman's senatorial colleague, Bennett Clark maintained Reed's record of obsessive opposition to governmental expansion. It remained for Truman to harmonize Missouri's venerable skepticism and the fresh idealism of the Democratic party under Franklin D. Roosevelt, a task that required considerable ingenuity.

Like Benton, his great predecessor of a century before, Harry Truman revered the Jeffersonian concept of a simple, rural republic. Similarly, Truman admired the courage of their hero, Andrew Jackson, in battling the numerous enemies whom Truman was convinced were still perverting public interests for private advantage. Combining a keen appreciation of history and a shrewd grasp of the Missouri character, Harry Truman found himself in circumstances where he could serve America while proving himself to be the quintessence of Jeffersonian Missouri. Throughout his career, Harry Truman happily identified himself with Missouri, clearly believing there was something unique and valuable about his state.

Truman's forebears came to Missouri in the 1840s while Benton was enjoying his last successful years. With names such as Gregg and Young, well known back in Kentucky, these migrants headed for Jackson County, bringing with them their slaves to follow a life typical for that part of Missouri. They kept their interests essentially agricultural so that should occasional excursions into trade or speculation fail, the land was there to fall back upon. It was a family dedicated to the Democratic party, with the dexterity needed to move loyally and easily from Grover Cleveland to Bryan. In this manner both of

Harry Truman's grandfathers, Anderson Truman and Solomon Young, were prominent figures in southern Jackson County who made it clear that they and their kin were comfortable with the county's strongly Confederate traditions.

John Truman's son, Harry, was born in 1884, the same year the Democratic party won one of its two national victories between 1856 and 1912. There was something instructive about the career of John Truman, a good farmer whose attention seemed easily distracted from agriculture. He became quite successful as a trader, especially in mules, and was able to move his family to Independence. Young Harry thus grew up with mixed memories of farm and small-town life. In 1903 John Truman lost his modest resources after speculating on grain futures, which meant he was forced to give up Missouri soil settled by Truman ancestors in 1844. Nevertheless, with his son, Harry, John Truman retreated to the land, working the 600 acres near Grandview which Solomon Young, John's father-in-law, had nurtured so carefully. Although his father soon wandered off to be county road overseer, Harry Truman settled down to run the farm.

For eleven years Harry Truman thrived as a bookish, bachelor farmer, living with his family and becoming thoroughly grounded in the cautious outlook fostered by Jackson County's old Confederate spirit. He came to know the region well, an area so typical of the essential Missouri. Only the war in 1917 was able to take Truman away, perhaps because of the same allure which had prompted him once to seek admission to the military academy at West Point. After service in France Truman returned to Jackson County, considering himself much changed and with new ambitions. While the alteration may have seemed superficial, his life was profoundly different. The young farmer, now thirty-five years old, married Bess Wallace, a chum from school days, with the two joining Truman's mother-in-law in the large Wallace house in Independence which eventually became famous as the White House in Missouri. Inspired by new goals and his bride's reluctance to be a farmer's wife, Truman tried his hand at business. With luck no better than his father's,

Harry Truman soon seemed to be a failure in the world beyond the land.

In this setting, a bankrupt Truman entered Missouri politics, laboring for more than a decade within the Democratic organization of Jackson County. He served briefly as member from the rural eastern district on the body which managed county affairs, the Jackson County Court. After losing re-election, perhaps because of Ku Klux Klan opposition, Truman won again in 1926, this time as presiding judge of the county body. Thereafter, he was a brilliant success in stressing honest government, in providing efficient service, and in building durable and desperately needed roads. Undaunted by the 1929 crash, Truman became the principal voice for the Democrats in the region surrounding Kansas City. However, it was a voice within a system controlled by Tom Pendergast: Truman's ties with the machine had become obvious since he had entered the organization through the promptings of Mike and Jim Pendergast, brother and nephew of the man whom Truman recognized as the "Big Boss."

In 1934 Tom Pendergast needed a candidate to represent the machine in that year's Senate race. As third choice, Harry Truman found himself struggling for a seat in the Senate rather than for a place in the House of Representatives, which he preferred. In addition to his much-admired record as a county administrator, Truman showed he had considerable capacity for speaking the Missouri political language. His familiarity with the farm plight, his use of the rural vernacular, and his simplistic division of the world into good guys and bad guys made it possible for Truman to win a narrow primary victory. He drew surprising support, as one newspaper put it, from the people at the creek forks and grass roots. Stumping Missouri in the astounding heat of 1934, Truman devised a campaign style of neighborliness and candor which he would use in the other significant contests of his career—when he fought stubbornly for re-election in 1940, and in 1948, when he won probably the most surprising victory in presidential politics.

Harry Truman, with his Missouri qualities, quietly flourished in the United States Senate. Despite the handicap of association with a political machine soon unveiled as a state and national disgrace, Senator Truman moved along the path he had followed as a county judge. He talked in Washington of simplicity and efficiency in government. He warned against the ease with which wealth could take advantage of the farmer and the working man. At the same time, he displayed such loyalty to the Democratic party as to support President Roosevelt's controversial plan to enlarge membership on the Supreme Court. Most significant, perhaps, was the new senator's immediate display of the traditional Missouri suspicion of power and size in high place, whether in economics or politics.

Because of this outlook Truman won the significant friendship of the nation's most distinguished Jeffersonian liberal, Louis D. Brandeis, associate justice of the Supreme Court. Brandeis especially admired Truman's attack on the menace and the ineffectiveness of the country's transportation behemoths. While Brandeis's St. Louis association was perhaps too brief to make him an authentic Missouri son, he and Truman seemed to form a natural intellectual alliance. Like Brandeis, Truman found himself obliged to accept the exercise of governmental power in behalf of citizens dwarfed by business consolidation within the Republic's economy. In this spirit Truman learned to use political power in a fashion appropriate for a Missouri Jeffersonian.

While still an obscure senator, Truman became chairman of a congressional committee charged with examining honesty and efficiency in the defense and war efforts by America's industrial-corporate giants. This group, which in time came to be known as the Truman Committee, disclosed repeatedly what most Missourians would have predicted—that the inhabitants of the industrial and commercial world could not be trusted even in time of national peril. Truman and his committee colleagues reputedly saved the American people billions of dollars by uncovering the waste, corruption, and ineffectiveness regularly found in the realm of banks and industry. This success reflected the tough skepticism which experience had bred into Truman's state. It was hardly surprising, therefore, that when the Missouri senator was chosen by Franklin Roosevelt to be the vice-presidential candidate in 1944, the conservative community exulted.

As president, Harry Truman was never far from the farms and small towns of Missouri nor from the simplistic political creed which flourished there. Unlike Benton, Truman was always eager to escape Washington and took every chance to fly back to Independence, borne in a presidential plane named after his home town. Truman's relaxed walks around Independence, which were possible in the casual days before President Kennedy's assassination and national television, made him the last of the village presidents, in the sense that he embodied the spirit of small-town America. His preferences in language and anecdote also made him the last of the dirt farm presidents. After Franklin Roosevelt's death, Truman's first inquiry to reporters was whether they knew what it was to have a bull or a hay pile fall on them. In 1948 he told America he was summoning Congress to a special session beginning on Turnip Day, an occasion known to all dedicated Missourians as the only time to plant turnips. In the battle later that year to be elected president in his own right, Truman did as Benton had done a century earlier; he went forth to talk to the people at railroad crossings, in the hamlets, and even in city auditoriums.

Although his style and efforts were ridiculed in 1948 until the morning after the election day, Truman's preaching in the colorful Jeffersonian language of Missouri wove a charm. His manner from the famous rear platform of his campaign train was much that of a Missouri farmer visiting with his neighbors. Truman did nothing unusual at the whistle-stops, only what he had done for more than a decade in the Senate—assail America's concentrated wealth, with its retinue of bankers and lawyers. His words and his spirit were reminiscent of Andrew Jackson's messages on the Bank of the United States and the specie question, speeches written by Thomas Hart Benton. His use of the language of Bryan and Jackson seemed somehow reassuring to a nation fumbling in a baffling postwar world. Apparently this effect was little diminished by critics who charged that Truman's simplifications issued only from the instinctive conservatism of a country man bred in Missouri.

In approaching the issues and the people, Truman never displayed the slightest misgiving over whether he might be short-sighted or wrong. He simply explained to his friends, the people, how sinful were their enemies—all the privileged interests which threatened the farmers and workers of Missouri and everywhere. Despite the fact that many newspapers tried to give Truman's entourage a reputation as country bumpkins, Truman persisted in summoning his listeners to join on the side of the oppressed against the privileged few. Millions of voters were somehow cheered when Truman called himself a country boy.

Actually, Truman thought a great deal about the historical underpinnings beneath the challenge he had offered the American people in 1948. His *Memoirs* bristle with expressions of devotion to Thomas Jefferson and Andrew Jackson and the belief that the Democrats stood for the beleaguered common man. Conversely, Truman delighted in arguing that the Republican party was the refuge for selfish and wealthy interests. He talked of how Jackson's victories had restored the liberalism of Jefferson against "the forces of reaction." Jefferson had defeated "those who controlled the land and the banks." In restoring this victory, Jackson "represented the interests of the common people of the United States." Furthermore, Truman admiringly insisted that Jackson had made clear to America what was right and who was wrong. Truman had no difficulty seeing that evil was the "moneyed interests of the conservative East." [1]

Carrying Missouri's political instincts to Washington proved to have its difficulties for President Truman. The earnest loyalties of appointees and confidantes toward Truman and vice versa produced what some persons called his "Missouri Gang," whose antics caused some national distress and bemusement. Beyond being personally embarrassed by several of his oldest Missouri friends, Truman never was quite successful in shaking

1. Harry S. Truman, *Memoirs, Years of Trial and Hope,* 2 vols. (Garden City, N.Y.: Doubleday, 1956–1957), 1:172–173, 193–195.

the stigma of association with the Pendergast machine as well as his later involvement with St. Louis Democratic powers. More significant, perhaps, was that Truman came to experience Benton's difficulty as he too faced circumstances which eventually obliged him to take a stand somewhat against the outlook in Missouri.

Truman's insistence that civil rights must be guaranteed to black Americans conflicted with much of the sentiment in Missouri. As late as 1940, Senator Truman had been content to say that only justice was needed for the Negro, and that social equality was no one's goal. America was much different a decade later, although Truman's advocates insisted that his astonishing presidential recommendations were still in Missouri character. His fight for the black citizens' civil rights, his pleas for health insurance, his call for more public-owned power, and his efforts to enlarge support for the farmer were justified by his supporters as necessary government moves in behalf of the dignity and freedom of the citizen. This paradox in Harry Truman's executive policies was as old as Thomas Jefferson's own administration.

Harry Truman retired to Missouri, remembered not for his limited attainment in domestic legislation or for his larger achievement in foreign affairs, but for his success in demonstrating that politics in modern America could be tamed by the man on the farm or on the street. Through Truman's capacity to convert complex issues into simplifications and to make it appear easy to identify right from wrong, America was briefly tempted to envision a restoration of the old Republic. However, not long after the miraculous campaign of 1948, many citizens seemed to tire of the old Missouri calls to battle against the venerable evils which President Truman always seemed to be fighting.

Not until after his death did Harry Truman become a folk hero to America, a remarkable thing for an obscure county politician once ridiculed by opponents as errand boy for Tom Pendergast. One of the largest selling books of the 1970s was a compilation of conversations with Truman which disclosed vividly his Missouri conservatism, expressed in the former president's pithy language. At the same time, the interpretations of distinguished actor James Whitmore of Truman soliloquizing came to rival the wide appeal of Hal Holbrook's famed impersonation of Sam Clemens. For this role Whitmore received an Academy Award nomination in 1976 for "Best Actor." On stage and on television, it seemed that bicentennial America's search for the old verities found considerable comfort in the expostulations of these two colorful Missourians.

While Truman usually managed to find common ground for his Missouri values and the national challenges, to his frequent discomfort Missouri herself seemed increasingly troubled by the course of American affairs. The profound issues of the years after 1920 coaxed only a limited and reluctant appreciation from Missouri. At times she seemed almost pathologically negative. The ancient rural conservatism remained steadfast while in the cities the Democrats were the playthings of powerful political machines whose success renewed questions about the role of government and the virtue of cities.

Despite the fact that there were three Republican governors in the 1920s, Missouri gradually awarded the Democrats a mastery in state affairs which exceeded even the party's authority during Benton's time. It was a curious control, however, since the Democrats were usually divided, confused, and often spectacularly inept. Nevertheless, at the local level, most citizens remained comfortable with the party which had usually represented concerns of Missourians for more than a century. On the two occasions after 1928 when Missouri chose Republican governors, in 1940 and 1972, it seemed that the Democrats were determined to give the office away. Somehow the state's deep-rooted commitment to limited government kept the Democrats in power, despite the party's lackluster leadership which was itself a reflection of Missouri's skepticism about politics and politicians.

With this debilitating public philosophy, Missouri's attempt to find dynamic uses in the old Jeffersonian orthodoxies became very difficult. Except for mild enthusiasm over better roads, if only to assure the new free rural mail delivery, Missouri either rejected or followed reluctantly most of the solutions which the federal government claimed were needed for serious problems. Whether in popular referenda or in the usually petty-minded general assembly, Missouri managed to thwart or delay important change. In the 1920s citizens turned aside efforts to reorganize government and to improve the constitution, while they allowed ancient localism to stifle efforts for a more equitable property tax system. As a result the desperate needs of education especially suffered.

In the 1920s Missourians seemed occupied with surviving agricultural depression, and after 1929 economic anxiety overcame all parts of the state's society. However, economic decline did not stampede the legislature, many of whose members found the prospect of more energetic government a graver threat than the depression. Only vehement insistence and even threats from Washington bureaucrats brought the general assembly reluctantly to undertake to pay for its share of the early New Deal relief measures. Eventually, of course, the New Deal era in Missouri brought the state to accept some change. Aid to elderly citizens, some improvement in health services, and tax increases were only part of the record. Meanwhile, the frauds which had come to be considered as normal in the urban centers were discovered moving into the capitol at Jefferson City, so that Missourians, made skittish by New Deal political vigor, had fresh proof of untrustworthy government. As one alternative, many Missouri farmers began co-operating for the sake of their special interests. The rise to power of the Missouri Farmer's Association and the Missouri Farm Bureau Federation was an indication of how a more militant sense of diversity within the state's interests could sometimes spur action beyond Jefferson City and occasionally even in Washington, D.C.

These divisions and the state's traditionally skeptical outlook allowed restraint to stay in command when Missouri finally replaced the constitution of 1875. Beginning in September 1943 and meeting for a year, a constitutional convention sat in a mood which was a distillation of Missouri caution. Dominated by the certainty of members that any innovative document was doomed, the delegates carefully steered away from issues which might enlarge the bitter relationship between the two cities and the countryside. These delicate arrangements contrived to bury many important questions, ultimately permitting an obviously pleased presiding officer to predict at the convention's close that the proposed document would gratify the state's composite view. Missouri's Jeffersonian mistrust of government was evident in the new constitution, which proved to be a classic restatement of nineteenth-century political philosophy.

Efforts to move a number of executive officials from an elective to an appointive basis were defeated, leaving the executive branch still comprising what often was called a cabinet of little governors. The only significant increase in the governor's power was in budget management. In the general assembly no change was made which might noticeably alter the deeply rural spirit of that body. In the judicial branch the new constitution managed to transform Missouri's cautious spirit into a virtue. A scheme was incorporated which gave voters regular opportunity to remove judges from the major benches. This nonpartisan court plan drew national attention and emulation. As for local government, the convention found the issue too volatile for safety and agreed that such matters should be decided by the general assembly. Left in place, therefore, were the 345 township units, relics of Missouri's glorious past. In short, the new constitution differed little with its predecessor of 1875.

While 60 percent of the populace voting was willing to accept the constitution in the 1945 referendum, only one out of five eligible voters took the trouble to express a view. Agreement was not universal, despite the convention's caution, for much of rural Missouri felt the document threatened too much change. In many remote counties the voters rejected the proposal, summoned to opposition by carefully spread rumors that the new constitution would force white and "colored" children to share schools. In fact, the constitution clearly called for separate schools for "white and colored" children unless the law provided otherwise. This proviso merely meant that Negro children in those districts where the black population was tiny might be permitted to go to the school for the white majority if local sentiment was willing.

Thus a new constitution came into being, prepared by a convention whose very calling seemed so delicate a matter that Gov. Forrest Donnell, with marvelous Missouri caution, refused to approve or oppose the issue. In 1845 the state house of representatives had been the great bastion for tradition and for the rural viewpoint. In 1945 Missourians saw to it that this situation was little changed, leaving the character of the state's government much as it had been in the height of the Jackson era. The 1945 constitution had its own longevity, for it was still securely in place in 1976. By then it had been modestly altered by amendment, but it stood steadfast, like most citizens who were waiting to be shown some virtue in the age of innovation. Missouri's reaction to the changing American imagination was still profoundly shaped by her cherished Jeffersonian legacy. The state continued to pit rural forces against the city, ancient political alliances against contemporary pressure, and caution against action.

9

America in Missouri's Imagination

*T*HE persistence of a Jeffersonian spirit in Missouri's politics during the century after 1876 was only the most obvious
manner in which the state's imagination responded to the changing character of the nation. Missouri found it increasingly difficult to be a companion in the federal Union which emerged
after the Civil War. The forces newly at work in America
seemed to accept the inevitability and desirability of consolidation, whether in government, business, agriculture, or in
human relations. In thus discarding Jeffersonian goals, the nation hastened after a society of giant cities, corporate agriculture, business goliaths, and an enormous government. Deeply
disturbed by these developments, Missouri tried either to endure
the changes or to take refuge in skepticism and intransigence.

Only briefly had Missouri seemed to keep pace with the new
American spirit. In 1872 Gov. Gratz Brown sought the presidency and Missouri's Liberal Republican movement challenged
America to re-embrace old values. At that time some persons
thought a new tide of immigration might invigorate the state.
Sam Clemens created the delightful rascal, Colonel Beriah
Sellers, to express the enthusiasm of some Missourians in the
1870s. The fast-talking Sellers, in *The Gilded Age,* wrote to
eager friends in Tennessee:

> Come right along to Missouri! Don't wait and worry about a good
> price but sell out for whatever you can get, and come along, or you

166

might be too late. Throw away your traps, if necessary, and come
empty-handed. You'll never regret it. Its the grandest country—the
loveliest land—the purest atmosphere—I can't describe It; no pen
can do it justice. And its filling up, every day—people coming from
everywhere.[1]

Clemens made Colonel Sellers stand for false prophecy and
poor judgment, just as Missouri found by 1880 that events were
weakening her famed vigor and charm. The state's disillusion
began where, curiously, her history had begun, which was with
the career of St. Louis. In its first century of life, Missouri's
proud metropolis had prospered while keeping its distance from
the state. After 1865 St. Louis became preoccupied with the
conviction that its future rested in a national rather than a state
or regional role. With one out of five Missourians living in St.
Louis, many of these residents accepted the talk that their town
had an extraordinary mission which had now transcended the
continent to become global. In the city's view, logic implied
that if Missouri had a glorious future, it was in endorsing the career of St. Louis, especially since the city expected to serve as
the new federal capital. St. Louisans also proudly emphasized
that their town was close to New York and Philadelphia in the
race to be the nation's manufacturing center.

One of the most ardent collaborations between material and
intellectual expectations was found in St. Louis during the
1870s. When Eads's great bridge crossed the Mississippi to welcome America to Missouri, the philosophers in St. Louis found
they could explain the city's destiny in spiritual terms. Thanks
especially to William T. Harris, Henry Brokmeyer, Denton J.
Snider, and their Philosophical Club, German philosophy taught
the global destiny of St. Louis. The dialectical process espoused
by Hegel, which Brokmeyer and others had been trying to share
with St. Louis, suddenly had a pertinent message. According to
those who followed Hegel's argument, progress emerged from
the synthesis of natural forces, which was supposed to make it
self-evident to believers that St. Louis was about to be the

1. Mark Twain and Charles Dudley Warner, *The Gilded Age,* 2 vols. (New York:
Harper, 1915), 1:13.

foremost result when freedom and material achievement were combined in America.

So intensely did some St. Louisans contend that their city was ordained for unlimited greatness that they hailed the tragic 1871 Chicago fire as the inevitable destruction of Missouri's antithesis. Whether at meetings of philosophers, bankers, or politicians during the 1870s, St. Louis repledged its faith that the map and the stars alike pointed to it as the logical new leader of America and perhaps the globe. This wide belief had been nourished by the thrilling 1870 volume entitled *St. Louis, the Future Great City of the World*. In it, Logan U. Reavis made the usually obscure Hegelian doctrines very clear on the point of St. Louis's evolution toward glory. Consequently, when delegates to Missouri's 1875 constitutional convention suggested St. Louis would be prudent to seek a more integrated role in state affairs, the city turned a deaf ear as it did to others who warned that eventually St. Louis would desperately need the patronage and sympathy of Missouri. Instead, the city made the national centennial era a time of preparation for becoming the new federal capital.

Disillusion came swiftly. On the eve of the cruelly revealing 1880 census, even America's poet of mystical nature and continental attainment, Walt Whitman, had difficulty understanding the city's expectations. Wandering along the riverfront, Whitman was stirred by the bustle as well as the looming presence of the Eads bridge. While he was pleased with the sensation of being at the continent's very center, Whitman saw St. Louis only as part of a greater entity, the central state of Missouri. Others who visited the city around 1880 had even more trouble recognizing any magisterial destiny for the area since they noticed the general unkemptness, the filth, the smoke, and the amazing number of brothels, all of which made St. Louis at best a very ragged child of destiny.

Then came the 1880 census report that Chicago, the detested foe, had quickly surpassed St. Louis in size and wealth. Had there been miscalculations about Missouri's future? This seemed impossible for many believers who preferred to accept rumors that the U.S. Bureau of the Census had been corrupted by enemies of St. Louis. Surely Logan Reavis's inspired book could not have been wrong in its forecast of ten million inhabitants for St. Louis? Although many citizens sought to remain faithful, St. Louis's prospects as a world center collapsed sadly after 1880, as the departure of some dynamic figures seemed to signify. Gen. William Tecumseh Sherman had returned to his beloved St. Louis after the Civil War, where he remembered a city filled with frugal and industrious citizens. In 1886 Sherman reluctantly moved to New York City as a place better suited to his needs. Five years later, he was brought back for burial.

Meanwhile, other energetic citizens abandoned St. Louis. The organizer of Hegelian philosophy and city education, William T. Harris, headed for larger opportunities in the East. Joining him was Joseph Pulitzer, who did leave some of his feverish self behind in his newspaper, the *Post-Dispatch*, which became the state's finest journal and one of the great papers in the United States (although Missourians rarely heeded its emphasis on public quality and progress). Before moving away, Pulitzer had the courage to point out how St. Louis was rapidly slipping from the high pinnacle it claimed in national affairs. Carl Schurz gave up hope abruptly, once he lost his Senate seat. When his service as President Hayes's secretary of the interior was finished in 1881, Schurz discovered he could not be happy returning to St. Louis for a career in letters so he joined the trek to New York City, where he preached reform as a journalist and author.

These emigrés found themselves far indeed from St. Louis, where political and environmental pollution were left to take command, and especially from the rural reaches of Missouri which could have profited enormously from their energy and brilliance. Their flight signaled how the great illusions of St. Louis were fading. Within twenty years the glamor was gone and Missouri was left to deplore the new reputation St. Louis was acquiring for dishonor and squalor. Rapidly, St. Louis grew infamous for its tenements, filth, violence, and corruption. Not even the Hegelian philosophers could have brought comfort when the city experienced in 1900 a terrible street car operators' strike in which fifteen men were slain and many more injured while the St. Louis administration shrugged hopelessly. In this manner St. Louis earned the title of America's worst governed city. It was the first town to be assailed in one of America's most famous political tracts, Lincoln Steffens's *Shame of the Cities*. It was also the only town in very unsavory company to be attacked a second time by him.

Steffens and other critics were particularly struck by the way in which some of St. Louis's and Missouri's political and cultural leaders appeared oblivious to the city's deterioration. They marveled that some St. Louis spokesmen could still boast about their town, despite the ghastly conditions of its jails and hospitals, and the fact that the drinking water seemed to be liquid mud. Steffens praised Circuit Attorney Joseph Folk's crusade for especially showing how vestrymen, social leaders, teachers, and many other notable St. Louis groups could be complacent abettors of their city's moral and physical collapse. Beyond this, Steffens was simply aghast that St. Louis citizens could not be shamed. His second essay on the city stressed that, despite its exposure as a community that was dirty, sick, and despoiled, St. Louis went calmly on with business. Steffens also pointed to the spreading decay of government across Missouri, noting the state's supreme court had managed to overturn the conviction of Joe Folk's chief target, the boss of St. Louis, Edward Butler.

Such observations touched upon the real plight of both St. Louis and Missouri early in the twentieth century. Gone were the impulses for growth, change, or reform. Cynicism and indifference seemed to supplant the hopeful energies of Gratz Brown's era and the optimistic expectancy of the Hegelians. When a civic league was founded in St. Louis in 1902, it was generally regarded as an elitist effort to protect special interests. The city's attitude became increasingly fragmented and suspicious, with residential segregation being established on the eve of World War I. Earnest efforts by Roger Baldwin, a Washington University professor of sociology who fought for civic rejuvenation, salvaged pride among some circles in 1914. However, most of the city's heterogeneous social and economic elements were left unmoved as well as untouched. The city seemed adrift.

Time grew no kinder to St. Louis nor to Missouri. Many St. Louis citizens after World War I seemed content to think that the Democratic machine rising in Kansas City was more odious than the one in St. Louis. Observers tended to find the city cruel, sordid, and utterly commercial. Meanwhile, the town coughed through a deepening smoke crisis until action was forced in 1939 by the smoke abatement crusade. After St. Louis endured twenty consecutive days of lung-rending, eye-searing smog, the cheap, impure coal from nearby southern Illinois was finally banned. Although the smoke somewhat cleared, the city's circumstances grew worse while citizen apathy increased. The independent status and boundaries acclaimed in 1875 began to strangle the city: an urban kingdom once hailed as adequate for eternity had not sufficed for a century.

Surrounded by catastrophe, between 1947 and 1953 the community calmly voted down proposals for five different bond issues. In 1950 a new charter was rejected. An effort to obtain important school bonds was defeated in 1951, and a similar fate overcame a redevelopment proposal in 1953. Such fiscal restraint suggested that St. Louis citizens were not so very different after all from their fellow Missourians outstate. A kind of nadir was reached in 1951 when a new executive, on being transferred to St. Louis to take command of a major firm, bluntly announced that he was moving into a decadent city. Comments like this and stern reproaches from the *Post-Dispatch* finally stirred enough citizens after 1953 for an attempt at renewal. Raymond R. Tucker, an engineering professor at Washington University, won election as a mayor dedicated to revive the inert town.

For a time there was vitality on the banks of the Mississippi. Bond issues were approved, as were an earnings tax and redevelopment plans. National magazines soon featured St. Louis as a case study in treating urban disease. A new baseball stadium and the Saarinen arch for the Jefferson memorial became pledges that St. Louis was determined to escape its past. An enormous housing development for low-income families, the Pruitt-Igoe project, was considered even more serious proof of the city's attempt to face its problems. Amid these ventures, entertainment centers and handsome apartment towers replaced older, dingy settings, thereby inviting spirited citizens to return and enjoy life in St. Louis.

The revival was brief. Early in the 1970s, Pruitt-Igoe stood empty, a desolate expanse of buildings which America pondered as an error in concept and design, while ventures into luxurious shopping and dwelling centers were bankrupt. Mayor Tucker had been succeeded by politicos whose presence reminded some citizens of the dreary circumstances in the 1930s. By 1976, the town's peak population of 880,000 had dwindled to less than 500,000, a striking indication of the fact that between 1960 and 1970 alone, St. Louis's population had been diminished by 17 percent. This population loss meant that along with its other dubious achievements, old St. Louis had become the outstanding American instance of outward dispersal of people from a decaying central city, so that a community remained whose child-bearing capacity was shrinking and whose fiscal resources were dwindling. St. Louis in the 1970s was literally a crisis in human dependence and poverty, while the wealthy St. Louis County— so haughtily brushed aside by the city in 1875—stood nearby in relative comfort. There were signs in 1976 that the many small surrounding communities might somehow promote a revival of St. Louis, with the goal of making the old city a habitable business center into which county residents could come each day for work and vanish with nightfall.

To the chagrin of many Missourians, St. Louis's desperate plight after 1970 was given careful attention and wide publicity when the RAND Corporation received a million dollars from the National Science Foundation to perform what was generally considered to be an autopsy on the town. Why St. Louis had deteriorated at such a spectacular rate became a national question. Some city leaders argued that this was a wasted inquiry, insisting that plans for new business and a convention center proved that St. Louis was still alive and well. The findings of the RAND study disproved this thesis, bringing cries that short-sighted investigators had used evidence drawn from the wrong people. Certainly the opinion of the RAND project was cruel and cutting. It advised St. Louis city to forget its ancient prominence and to accept a modest role as only one among many communities in the larger association of metropolitan St. Louis. This investigation thus pronounced the death of St. Louis, a city which the Hegelians once had claimed was becoming the center of the earth. The sword of materialism had cut two ways, St. Louis discovered.

However, not even its dismal fate seemed to alter St. Louis's disdain for most things Missourian. St. Louis might be *in* Missouri, but it evidently felt little need to be *of* Missouri. Actually, the larger meaning of St. Louis's decline was its exemplification of what happened generally in Missouri during the century after 1875. The experience of St. Louis as it fell into mortal illness profoundly impressed the state, at which point her longstanding caution and skepticism came into good use. Missouri at large had far fewer expectations than once had cheered St. Louis. Still, there was concern and resentment across the state over her changing relationship with the nation. To fall behind her early pace was disquieting, but the challenge to Missouri's self-esteem was much more profound than merely one of comparative size.

In 1880 Missouri learned that the number of her farmers who were forced to accept tenant status had risen beyond the national average. This was grave news for a state which had long revered the ideal of a land dominated by independent farmers. Further distress came from changes in the patterns of American transportation. Missouri's economy as well as her stature had from the start been buoyed by the knowledge that national movement would necessarily pour through the state. Cruel changes in America's lines of motion as well as the shift of interest toward city life subordinated Missouri physically, and inevitably helped to subdue the state's mood. Most Missourians, however, were clearly reluctant to hasten after new national fashions. The distressing decline seemed rather to bolster the state's determination after 1880 to preserve the traditional Missouri.

Long after agriculture's dominance had begun to weaken, Missouri continued to represent herself as a farmer's kingdom, a habitual practice for a state determined to carry on Senator Benton's crusade in behalf of the simple, independent farmer. Missouri had cheered when Benton fought to give small farmers public land at little or no cost. Into the twentieth century the general assembly kept the faith by issuing self-serving descriptions of Missouri as a special place where the poor man might escape tenancy and be lifted to the independence which, as Jefferson had taught, came only with the possession of tillable soil. As late as 1925, Jackson County's official literature talked about an idyllic garden seemingly unchanged from Josiah Gregg's rapturous descriptions of nearly a century before. No matter what Missouri wanted to believe, however, the yeomen farmers were leaving Missouri's soil. In Howard County, one of the earliest and most appealing agricultural areas, perhaps 13,000 citizens were fully occupied as farmers around 1880. By 1960 fewer than 6,500 lived outside the towns, and most of these persons were only occasional farmers.

Serious difficulties for Missouri agriculture became general in the 1870s. Before then Missouri had flourished by hard work, producing corn, wheat, garden produce, hemp, cotton, flax, tobacco, and grapes. Livestock had been plentiful. After 1860, when nearly half of Missouri's land was cultivated, the Civil War intruded to reduce much of this abundance, especially in southern and western Missouri where crops, buildings, and orchards were devastated, and machines and livestock were stolen. Despite remarkable restoration after 1865, agriculture was never again Missouri's proudly dominant way of life. There was growth until the rural population reached its highest point of 2 million in 1900, but at the same time the character of agriculture was changing. In 1880 nearly 75 percent of Missouri's people were rural; by 1910 this proportion had dropped to 57 percent.

Civil warfare was not the only chilling hand to be laid upon agriculture in Missouri. Along with farmers in other states, many Missourians were tempted away from subsistence agriculture by town and city markets, especially since the new machinery made large-scale production appear easy and indebtedness even easier. Quickly, the typical Missourian found himself divested of much of his valued independence, for by trying to make agriculture a business rather than a heroic adventure, he found himself battling a new version of an old enemy, financial privilege. Instead of Northern troops or Southern bushwhackers, the foes became railroad rates and mortgage agents, along with food processors and distributors. When large acreages were tilled, it was not by Jefferson's stouthearted yeomen, but by corporations and companies. The pattern was starkly evident to those who watched the 260,000 Missouri farms of 1920, which averaged 132 acres, decrease by 1975 to 175,000, with an average size of 235 acres. Of the million and a half farmers in 1975, close to one-half worked away from their land at least a hundred days annually.

Though Missouri's public spirit may have remained appropriate for a people of small farms, in 1970 nearly three-fourths of Missouri's citizens lived in towns and cities. Even so, the advantages of large-scale tillage continued to make the state important in American agriculture. In 1975, Missouri ranked second among the states in number of farms, including those specializing in hogs and beef. She was the foremost grower of many kinds of seeds, and stood fourth in production of cattle, calves, hogs, soybeans, and American cheese. Missouri was the sixth largest producer in hay, eighth in corn, and tenth in milk. This record meant that in 1975, activities related to agriculture involved one out of every five Missourians, and agribusiness created a third of the state's personal income. The state had maintained her tradition of variety, taking pride in raising nearly everything from alfalfa to zinnias.

Keeping her self-esteem rooted in agriculture, it was plausible that Missouri's enthusiasm for industry and commerce languished, giving her only a distant interest in the maturing of a modern economy. Missourians tended to peer fearfully from the fields, hills, and forests as the nation's economic trends after 1875 challenged the state's old ways. America's twentieth century growth offered few conditions in which Missouri could give national leadership. Uninterested in the rise of technology, the state settled mostly for efforts in producing raw materials, processing, assembling, and distribution. Nevertheless, Missouri's very size, location, and wealth lent her a modest place in the changed order, so that after World War II agriculture was deposed as the state's largest employer.

In 1975 one out of four Missourians not on the farm worked in manufacturing. These half-million employees were scattered widely, for the state was even here true to her tradition of variety. No industrial classification claimed more than 16 percent of the manufacturing force. The largest occupation was in assembling automobiles, where Missouri stood nationally second only to Michigan. Electrical equipment and supplies, food processing, apparel, paper and printing, machinery, and metal products were all significant employers, and in St. Louis County the aerospace industry was especially important. The ancient practice of mining, however, by 1975 required less than 1 percent of the state's nonagricultural workers. Even so Missouri continued as the world's leading producer of lead, supplying about 80 percent of America's needs alone. There was also production of iron, zinc, barite, coal, aluminum, cement, lime, and clay.

When the state's official literature tried to describe how Missouri fitted into an America of the 1970s, the distance between the state and the national imagination was exploited as an advantage. Missouri seemed to argue in her own behalf that somehow the citizens would cling to their old virtues while playing host to the factories and businesses of the new American order. The Missouri worker was thus presented as unusually diligent and stable. According to one official statement, "Perhaps it is Missouri's rich agricultural heritage that causes our people to consider work as a way of life, not just a burden." [2] These toilers were also pictured as willing to work harder for less, for it was clear that production employees in Missouri were paid beneath the national hourly average wage, and that those wages increased slower than the nationwide rate.

Missouri's announcement that she could co-operate with na-

2. From *Missouri*, a booklet replete with copies of Thomas Hart Benton's paintings and distributed in 1976 by the Missouri Division of Commerce and Industrial Development. It includes no pagination, nor are a place and date of publication indicated. Hereafter cited as *Missouri*.

tional economic trends while remaining uncontaminated was especially useful in her boasts about tax conditions. In trying to attract industry and business, the state drew more attention to her hospitable revenue system that she did even to the sterling, wholesome, and archaic virtues of the people in their beautiful countryside. Missouri's historic determination that few taxes were needed to keep a state alive was converted into a prime reason for new commercial and manufacturing firms to settle in the state. Corporate leaders were told by the state that "Missouri's concern for industry is exemplified by the fact that we get only 4.32 percent of our tax revenue from the corporate income tax. Only seven states with a corporate income tax get less of their revenue from this source." In pointing out that very modest taxes of any kind were levied in Missouri, the state's literature emphasized one of the attributes which Missourians had perpetuated while most of America proceeded differently. In Missouri, it was proudly said, "Both state and local government strive for a policy of tax restraint." [3]

This was no exaggeration. In the 1970s, as in the 1830s, Missouri's general assembly seemed determined that the state's participation in a changing Union should cost the citizens relatively little. In 1970 only five states extracted a lower per capita contribution from their citizens. Nevertheless, Missouri struggled to maintain an educational system, roads, parks, hospitals, and even welfare assistance programs. Given the state's reluctance to tax herself, thoughtful persons tempted by Missouri's propaganda were prone to question the quality of services in a state so far behind the national effort. Whatever the measure, Missouri's presence in modern America was often awkward.

Missouri's reluctance to share the American imagination persisted despite the attempts of several notable citizens to persuade the state to put aside her "show-me" skepticism. Among those who wanted Missouri to do more than drift behind national change were four remarkable persons. James S. Rollins, a cultivated gentleman politician, worked in behalf of education and the arts. Milton J. Turner tried to make Missouri a place of

3. *Missouri.*

opportunity for blacks. Norman J. Colman attempted to strengthen agriculture as a modern economic and moral force in Missouri. William Rockhill Nelson used journalism to encourage progress in western Missouri. Each of these four fell short in prodding Missouri toward a distant goal, yet each left the state with a slightly enlarged outlook on progress.

Perhaps James S. Rollins never fully succeeded in Missouri politics because he preferred the cosmopolitan views of the Whigs, a stigma hard to lose. As an attorney in Boone County he battled for many causes, including the use of public funds to strengthen the University of Missouri. Rollins was active through most of the nineteenth century and died in 1888 surrounded by evidence that his beloved Missouri was no longer a national leader. To the end of a long life, Rollins embodied the dynamic potential of early Missouri. What distinguished him from his neighbors was his persistent willingness to move beyond the point where the state's comfortable inclinations often tempted her to linger. His prestige was especially strong in the central river counties which Rollins used as a base in his struggles for a more mature state economy.

As a youth Rollins decided that Jacksonian localism was regressive so that in 1836, at the age of 24, he went on a trip with Edward Bates and Hamilton Gamble to Washington to represent Missouri's modest interests in railroads. For the next twenty years Rollins was a power in Missouri's Whig party, an affiliation which did not keep him from making two good runs for the governorship in 1848 and 1857. In losing the governor's chair by 300 votes in 1857, Rollins enjoyed his finest hour. He had sought to found an American party in Missouri, but not as a tool for intolerance as it was in many eastern states. Rollins hoped that this ill-fated movement might offer the way for moderate Democrats and Whigs to unite. Using his capacity to peer above the quagmire of politics, Rollins kept insisting that Missouri was strategically positioned to show America a new basis for public endeavor. Toward that end he tried to build a partnership between Whigs and Benton Democrats, only to be undone by Benton's own intransigence.

Contending strenuously for the Union, for a halt to slavery's

growth, and for moderation and reconciliation after the Civil
War, Rollins never lost his belief that Missouri's future strength
rested in co-ordinated use of her varied interests and talents.
This conviction was evident in his pro-Union contributions during 1860 and 1861 and in his work as a congressman during the
Civil War. By 1866 Rollins was moving into alliance with the
Democrats, a price he was willing to pay to forestall the divisive
tactics of Charles Drake's policies of hate. Earlier, his opposition to Drake's 1865 constitution had nearly succeeded in defeating the document.

On the whole, Rollins was rarely successful as a politician in
getting Missouri to think of future possibilities rather than ancient orthodoxies, but when he assumed another role his work
for Missouri prospered by comparison. Across most of his life
James Rollins tried to persuade Missourians that it was in their
best interest to support generously one public university. After
assuring that such an institution was placed in his own town of
Columbia where he could personally serve as its guardian, Rol
lins tried to build a reasonable financial basis for the university.
Long frustrated in securing public funding, Rollins finally took
a seat in the state senate after the Civil War in order to command efforts to get an appropriation for the university. Meantime he continued to preside over the institution's board of cura-
tors. In thus shifting his hopes for a new Missouri from politics
to education, Rollins showed himself in a significant sense to be
one of Missouri's most ardent Jeffersonians.

The university was not always a willing agent for Rollins,
despite his solicitous friendship. He struggled to develop some
diversity in the institution's programs, and he was barely able to
preserve the important tradition of one institution by preventing
establishment of a separate campus for agricultural education.
When higher training for mining was needed, Rollins made certain that the location for this purpose, though ninety miles from
Columbia, was still under the university's management. Rollins
even persuaded George Caleb Bingham to accept a faculty appointment, so that briefly the studio arts thrived at the University of Missouri as at no other institution of the time.

Even with these heroic efforts, however, Rollins's university never became a dynamic part of the state's intellectual life. In part this failure resulted from Rollins's determination that the institution should be seated in the center of the state. This site separated the campus by more than a hundred miles from each of the state's two cities. St. Louis gave its intellectual allegiance to William G. Eliot's Washington University, to the Jesuits' St. Louis University, and to certain eastern citadels of learning. Kansas City, meanwhile, showed a distinct preference for the nearby University of Kansas. The University of Missouri was left lonely amid the lovely Boone County countryside. The school tried in time to use agricultural education and the state's growing interest in football competition to keep some part of Missouri's attention. Eventually, nearly a century after the state first bowed to Rollins's insistence upon a tax-supported university, Missouri established a campus of the university in each of the two cities. Although Rollins probably would have applauded the spirit of this venture, he would surely have deplored the fact that these urban campuses by 1976 had not received state funds adequate for any remarkable success.

Rollins's hope that Missouri might keep pace with the nation through education was shared by Norman J. Colman. The two men had worked together to persuade the state that general and agricultural education were better united than separated. Colman made a career of presenting agriculture as a dynamic way of life, serving with distinction as a farmer, publicist, administrator, and politician. Coming to Missouri in 1852, he succeeded as an experiment-minded agriculturalist dedicated to the belief that farming required an open, inventive mind, and expressed this creed in a highly popular journal, *Colman's Rural World*. Although his audience extended far beyond Missouri, Colman was an influential figure in the state through his two famous farms and his political work.

Colman's strategy was to persuade his neighbors that farming could be an ennobling as well as a profitable profession. Through this somewhat mystical approach he believed Missouri could become a revitalized state. In pursuing his goals, Colman's personal attainments were impressive. He sat in the general assembly, was elected lieutenant governor in 1874, and a decade later was summoned to Washington, eventually serving President Grover Cleveland as America's first secretary of agriculture. While in Washington Colman collaborated with another Missourian, Congressman William H. Hatch, to launch federal spending for agricultural research. The Hatch Act of 1887 created agricultural experiment stations across America whose purpose was to do what Colman preached was essential—enrich the careers of farmers by bringing them new knowledge.

Colman was also devoted to the farmer's success as a person. He brought the Grange to Missouri, seeing it as a valuable social and educational vehicle. However, he pleaded with agriculture not to separate itself from America's other interests by the formation of a farmers' political party. This caveat did not deter Colman himself from sternly rebuking all enemies of agriculture as he lectured widely, especially in his favorite setting, the state fair. The middlemen, the trusts, the packers, the gold bugs, wasteful farmers—all these drew his wrath, just as campaigns for better roads, government reform, free trade, and improved education gained his support. The old man's words were meaningful to all too few Missourians. Only education and research would bring state and national power to farmers, he said, while condemning political intrigues—a warning which, even from Norman Colman, was more than most rural Missourians could accept. Nevertheless, in his magazine and at the lectern, Colman preached this message until his death in 1911.

Where Colman hoped to awaken Missouri through enlightened agriculture, James Milton Turner worked for a new society which would accept an educated black citizenry. In 1840 Turner was born a slave in St. Louis County, where his father soon earned the family's freedom through veterinary practice. Young Turner managed to fulfill an intense dedication to education in spite of the difficulties presented by antebellum Missouri, even to the point, eventually, of attending Oberlin College. When the Civil War began, he left St. Louis to serve for the Union, and was wounded at Shiloh before returning to Missouri to lead in the Reconstruction campaign to award Negroes their rights. At this point Turner was obliged to tie his cause closely to politics, a tactic which ultimately lost him ground since he had no source of support except Charles Drake and his cohorts.

In addition to an association with the Radical Republicans, Turner did develop influence in Missouri by two other means. He was secretary of Missouri's Equal Rights League, in which role he stumped the state, and he was also an assistant state superintendent of schools, a capacity which let him establish and teach in schools at Kansas City and Boonville. In education one of Turner's lasting achievements was assisting in the creation of Lincoln University at Jefferson City. This institution was begun after the Civil War out of contributions from soldiers in the 62nd and 65th Colored Infantry, where Missourians predominated. As a result of hard work by Turner and others in 1870 the general assembly agreed to provide modest regular financial support for Lincoln if the school was dedicated to instructing black teachers for Negro students. Although state money was always scant, Lincoln University struggled to serve Missouri largely in this guise until marked changes in educational practices and social attitudes by the mid-twentieth century brought the school a larger role, which came to include white as well as black students.

J. Milton Turner sought equal rights for blacks, but he could see no plausible alternative to creation of a separate school system for Missouri's blacks. Segregated though it was, Missouri's educational program for Negroes, which Turner chiefly founded, was for a time an American leader. This success was severely diminished with the arrival of political bitterness and financial decay after 1875. In necessarily aligning himself with Charles Drake, Turner found his cause linked with that of harsh repression for all southern sympathizers. Temporarily it brought him great success as he organized blacks into voting blocs for Grant Republicanism. However, when the unpredictable Drake turned away from the uproar he had largely created in Missouri, Turner and the black political activists were left stranded. Their position, scarcely popular under the best of circumstances, suffered by the unpopularity of Drake's radicalism—even moderate

Missourians were offended by most things associated with Drake's views.

President Grant rescued Turner from an awkward personal plight by placing him among the first blacks to serve in America's diplomatic corps. Turner was sent to Liberia as United States minister. After this distinguished exile was ended, Turner returned to a Missouri where hardened attitudes made a renewed campaign for black rights hopeless even if he had had the stomach for battle. Turner became a businessman, leaving renewed vigor for the rights of Missouri's black citizens to await events after 1950. Then, with the brief promise displayed by Turner long past, white Missourians would have to be led by a new generation of blacks aided by a sympathetic federal government.

With some success, Rollins, Colman, and Turner each opposed Missouri's cautiousness and indifference. None of them, however, left as enduring a mark on the state as did William Rockhill Nelson. His story and the character of modern Kansas City were closely entwined. By 1920 most newcomers to Kansas City were astonished at what they saw. In a town famed for violence, boisterous greed, and political corruption, there were parks, boulevards, and fountains which made Kansas City one of the loveliest cities in the world. All this was largely the attainment of Nelson, who himself was something of a human miracle. His influence and wealth had been evident in Kansas City soon after he arrived from Indiana in 1880 to found a newspaper. From that year until his death in 1915, Kansas City's progress came about essentially because of the impatience, zeal, and dreams of William Rockhill Nelson and his *Kansas City Star*.

Using the *Star* and soon its morning counterpart, the *Times*, Nelson achieved three goals. He made himself a millionaire; he became the most influential figure in western Missouri; and he began the physical transformation of Kansas City. Nelson was more than aware of the appallingly raw character of that town in the 1880s. The kind of squalor which simply depressed such visiting investors as Charles Francis Adams II enraged Nelson.

Using his influence as a journalist and his money, he forced upon the city a program of municipal beauty which was nearly magical. Even crusty Adams acknowledged in one of his last visits that real improvement was evident in Kansas City, once a person escaped the hideous downtown and entered the residential areas. Nelson's plan for a majestic city lingered until after World War II when it was eclipsed by a mood of growth for growth's sake as new sections of Kansas City were opened.

On another level of achievement, however, the city, the state, and even the world could hardly forget the most enduring contribution that one Missourian ever made to satisfying the human need for beauty. Nelson left much of his huge fortune to be used for a collection of great paintings and for a splendid gallery to house this art. Aided by another bequest, this from Mrs. Mary Atkins, the William Rockhill Nelson Gallery of Art was opened in 1933 in Kansas City. As early as 1897 Nelson had been determined that Missouri should see the achievement of great artists, so that he acquired works for a seminal exhibition from Europe and opened the Western Gallery. Nearly eighty years later, in 1976, the Nelson Gallery had become one of the world's finest museums, both in its collection and in its stunning physical location amid the open land, winding boulevards, fountains, and trees—all contributions that Kansas City owed to Nelson.

Nelson was determined to rule people's lives, as well as enrich them, dominating his newspaper and his employees just as he towered in the city and the state. The *Star* was one of the first papers intended to have an impact through wide circulation, for Nelson pioneered in distributing a paper for two cents. His attitudes were generally conservative enough to please most Missourians, although he fervently supported Theodore Roosevelt's political rebellion. Mostly because the imperious Nelson wished it, Missouri had a delegation at the 1912 Bull Moose convention, despite the earnest opposition of Governor Hadley. Nelson's grip could readily be felt beyond the boundaries of Kansas City.

Although he was chiefly interested in transforming Kansas City, Nelson never lost a concern for agriculture and the needs of rural Missouri. His *Weekly Star* was a separate newspaper intended to instruct the farmer in self-improvement as well as in Nelson's interpretation of national affairs. Consequently, for many farmers of Missouri as well as for most citizens of Kansas City, William Rockhill Nelson was nothing less than an oracle who did not hesitate to announce what was right or wrong. Nelson showed great zeal in advancing the best interests of the area as he saw those interests, even if his zeal was marred at times by a spirit of tyranny. More than any other figure in Missouri's history, he demonstrated how one individual could be powerful in affecting the outlook of a city and a state.

Rollins, Colman, Turner, and Nelson each found that Missouri's imagination was slow to accept the new mood of America. As Nelson discovered, even so youthful a place as Kansas City did not escape the malaise which crept through Missouri in the twentieth century. With the rest of the state, Kansas City watched many expectations dwindle, including the fact—incredible to many natives—that by the 1970s, Kansas City was no longer a center for meatpacking. The stockyards were rarely full, Union Station was a massive place of quiet shadows rather than a bustling railhub of the nation, and the stores along the hilly downtown streets were mostly deteriorating or closed, losing to the competition of outlying commercial centers, many of them across the state line in Kansas. In addition, segregation in Kansas City contrasted sharply with its vaunted aspirations, and ironically, not far from the beautiful district where the Nelson Gallery stood was the black ghetto which in 1968 witnessed terrible nights of flames and violence.

Nevertheless, Kansas City's plight seemed to cause its citizens little chagrin. In its centennial celebration of 1950 the town congratulated itself with the self-conferred title of "city of the future," evidently taking no warning from the fact that St. Louis had proudly used the same title eighty years before. In 1976 Kansas City still looked out across the plains as if it had no past and few problems, while St. Louis faced the prospect of death and possible rebirth. The spirit of Kansas City suggested that only beginnings were important: the town appeared to run on sheer energy, an inchoate body driven by an assortment of forces. Yet Kansas City's worship of the future entailed oblivion of a difficult if relatively brief past. It also meant persuading America to dismiss such matters as Tom Pendergast in exchange for recognition that Kansas City sat, not on a desert's edge, but in the center of the world's greatest garden. Out of this perspective Kansas City wanted to hasten toward some future success.

It was a rush in which even by 1976 Kansas City had never paused long enough to foster an urban character beyond that of a restless plains city, eager to thrive. As a town always preparing for its still untransacted destiny, Kansas City replaced St. Louis as the most alien part of Missouri. During a period when Missouri's imagination had become restrained by sober appraisals of human nature and by disappointed dreams, Kansas City appeared determined to ignore the perspective of a state to which it was affixed by the merest geographic accident. If Kansas City seemed uncertain and defensive to some observers it was not because of the difficulties suffered in the century since 1876 but because of an impatience with the pace of affairs, an eagerness for quickened change. The town chose to stress that it and never St. Louis had always been intended as the nation's great inland city. Kansas Citians celebrated the fact that they commanded a 600-mile radius of countryside which produced approximately 90 percent of America's hogs, cattle, wheat, and soybeans, so that, it was assumed, eventually a hungry and grateful world must come to town. Thus, while Missouri struggled to keep her spirit after St. Louis had lost its being, Kansas City appeared still in search of a soul.

As Kansas City shuffled impatiently, Missouri's imagination grew increasingly occupied with defending things past and proven. Many colorful bits of evidence pointed to this resolve. Early in the twentieth century, as many western states embraced woman suffrage, Missouri refused to be greatly interested. It took an alliance with the enemies of saloons for the advocates of women's votes even to get the issue on the ballot in 1914. That year Missouri men went to the polls to decide whether Missouri women were capable of a share in Missouri politics. It had been argued that the sordid plight of St. Louis would have been prevented by women voters. Evidently the males of Missouri were unimpressed, for among those voting in 1914, fewer than 20 percent favored suffrage for the ladies.

Fifty years later, Missouri's intransigent majority again faced women's rights by rallying to the antiabortion cause. In a rare display of national leadership, Missouri passed a statute designed to challenge the Supreme Court's 1973 defense of abortion. In a major statement on 1 July 1976, the nation's highest court waved away Missouri's insistence that wives must have their husbands' consent, and young daughters that of their parents, before abortion was permissible. The Supreme Court also rejected other features of Missouri's statute, all of which were clearly designed to hamper a woman's choice of abortion.

The intensity of Missouri's feeling over abortion was only one display of the state's name in conservative causes. Missouri tradition pervaded one of the most deeply felt religious disputes in recent American history. In the 1970s the nation became aware of a schism in the Missouri Synod of the Lutheran Church. This body, which had become second-largest among the world's Lutheran groups and the ninth-largest Protestant denomination in America, extended far beyond the state where its headquarters and history were centered. Even so, the debate over theological doctrine and denominational politics which rent the synod seemed peculiarly appropriate for a Missouri setting. The synod, almost as old as the state, had never been comfortable with the twentieth century. At its venerable Concordia Seminary in St. Louis where German had been spoken until 1930, the intellectual outlook had been largely sectarian. The church believed in ministering to the soul and not in social concerns.

Missouri Synod's conservative message was sent forth to a huge international audience from St. Louis each Sunday by radio on "The Lutheran Hour," the envy of many other denominations. Yet despite an apparently enormous success, the synod finally broke over the kind of theology which ought to dominate the training of its ministers and thus the thoughts of worshippers. Within this conflict during the 1970s it was nearly impossible to find any Missouri Synod figure whose outlook was other than conservative or cautiously moderate. The quarrel lay between kinds of conservatism, a division also fundamental to the population of Missouri. In what some journalists called the "second Missouri controversy," the synod's most fundamentalistic forces won readily, with the result that some congregations agonizingly began to withdraw from the Missouri hierarchy and the bulk of the faculty at Concordia Seminary was ousted. The issue remained within a theological and social heritage hardly distinguishable from that of the synod's founders, who had first gathered around the Missouri hamlet of Altenburg 140 years before.

The abortion fight and the Lutheran dispute were merely two instances of how, in the 1970s, the Missouri imagination was loyal to traditional and tested viewpoints. During the past century the state had not often encouraged the national spirit of motion and change. Such ardent figures as Gratz Brown, James Rollins, and Herbert Hadley were rare, and even these men never stepped far from Missouri's beaten path. In recent years the chief gesture Missouri made was the occasional dispatch of a forward-looking United States senator to Washington where, after all, his enthusiasm could be expressed safely outside the state. The comparatively dynamic outlook of Thomas C. Hennings, Jr., Stuart Symington, and Thomas Eagleton, men hardly typical of Missouri's senators, did little to diminish the impression fostered by the state of a deeply cautious people clinging to ancient values against the displeasing momentum of history.

Clearly, most Missourians pushed aside the boasts about material leadership heard in Kansas City. Instead, the authentic Missouri responded to American trends after 1950 with the firm insistence, often expressed by members of the general assembly, that as for their state—"We don't want to be first!"

Conclusion

$\mathcal{M}$ISSOURI'S willingness to stand back while others rush ahead prompts some observers to dismiss her as a state which somehow faltered after a promising beginning. Evidence can be selected to show that the cautious spirit and ancient ways from the Ozark Hills, the farms and hamlets along the river valleys, and the rolling countryside have made Missouri an anachronism in the United States. However, there are signs in America's bicentennial era that Missouri may once again become a significant resource for the nation. The most obvious indication is that the state's mood and manner are a reminder of the sobering realities of history to a nation made forgetful by the illusions of supposedly unlimited growth.

To individuals who choose to evaluate the national quandary, Missouri history extends an invitation to restudy the cautious wisdom of early America. On a simple plane, Missouri's example offers an appealing primitivism like that displayed by Harold Bell Wright in his *Shepherd of the Hills*. On a profound level, salutary aspects of Missouri tradition are expressed in the widely influential books of one of the state's most distinguished sons, Reinhold Niebuhr. A theologian who grew up in a Missouri parsonage at the close of the nineteenth century and who was trained in the conservative outlook of the Evangelical Church's Eden Seminary at St. Louis, Neibuhr became one of the twentieth century's most respected commentators on national affairs. His voice handsomely represents Missouri speaking out of her unique history.

Among the most thoroughly Missourian in spirit of Niebuhr's writings was his powerful *Irony of American History*. Here, by emphasizing the distance which had grown between American principles and the nation's attainments, he urged that men not be deluded into ignoring this discrepancy. Niebuhr espoused Missouri doctrine when he recommended a skeptical approach to all things mortal. History, he said, taught the limits of man's nature and, consequently, the importance of foreseeing only modest results from human effort. Niebuhr's message was one which many thoughtful Missourians had long ago taken from the struggles of their state. He preached that while men ought of necessity to strive toward improvement, they should approach their work not with the expectation of certain progress and perfection, but with anticipations of error and folly. The striking feature of Niebuhr's distillation of the Missouri outlook was its resemblance to the viewpoint which actually had pervaded America in 1776 and for some decades thereafter. In the early Republic, talk of the inevitability of progress, the virtue of change, or the perfectibility of mankind was far more rare than modern Americans have recognized.

The admonitions from Jefferson's era, which most of Missouri's history sought to follow, recently began receiving wider national attention. In 1976 there have been indications that the old sobriety has been reviving when some Americans did not allow lessons from such experiences as Vietnam, Watergate, and environmental catastrophe to be entirely lost. If a renaissance of the spirit of Jefferson's age continues, the ordeal of Missouri could again be important to the nation. Toward that end, there are hints that Missouri might prove her ancient caution has not been wholly negative and paralyzing. For instance, Missouri has sought to preserve her cherished land, water, and wildlife and to foster agricultural education in a meaningful way. In the 1975 fiscal year, Missouri spent two and a half million dollars for environmental health, when a decade before, she had become a national leader in enacting pollution controls, especially for air quality. Similarly, the state moved decisively in 1973 to guard fish, wildlife, forests, and land by creating the State Environmental Improvement Authority. This agency could issue tax-free bonds or notes for projects to relieve pollution and solid waste difficulties.

With a lovely garden both as habitation and responsibility, latter-day Jeffersonians of Missouri seem to have sensed that this natural legacy required a serious political response. Although the state's official literature continues to intone the principles which had been fundamental to Missouri for nearly two hundred years, insisting "Missouri living is geared to the individual," the state has nevertheless recognized in one area that human well-being requires far-sighted restraints by the government.[1]

Beyond this regard for environmental security there have been other indications that Missouri caution had its fruitful side. While most of her county seats declined, an interesting alternative was rising. Population centers appeared in various parts of the state where regional needs for health, education, and commerce could be met in a contemporary manner without the blight of urban congestion. To centers such as Springfield–Joplin, Sikeston, Hannibal, Jefferson City–Columbia, and Chillicothe, many Missourians came for the advantages of modern America without the errors which St. Louis and Kansas City seemed to illustrate. These trends in turn helped persuade young Missourians to stay on the land in greater numbers in the 1970s than in previous decades. The state's newest generation appeared to find in farming some of the appeal it carried a century or more before. Several semirural areas of the state were among the fastest growing regions in the United States.

However, if Missouri's Jeffersonian perspective is to serve her and the nation into the twenty-first century, some serious problems remain to be faced. Above all, America needs to reconsider the essentials for a satisfactory life. It has long been apparent that what many Missourians sought from existence and what most Americans were pressured to expect from life are quite different. Here Missouri's history and spirit could prove

1. *Missouri* (Missouri Division of Commerce and Development, 1976).

significant in prompting the nation to substitute reasonable goals for the self-destructive pattern of haste, accumulation, and waste which captivates the national appetite. Just as important would be the creation in Missouri of a more congenial accord between all her citizens, whether they reside in Kansas City, in Taney County, in St. Louis, or in Howard County. A genuine unity in diverse Missouri could become the guide for a greater accord in America.

So, it remains to be seen whether this region, in which America's two greatest rivers meet, can recapture an important place in American development. Missouri's tough realism and Stoic candor have the potential to offer America some thoughtful restraints needed if democracy in the United States reasonably expects to survive a third century. Something more striking than mere statistical curiosity must soon come from the fact that during 1976 the continental center of America's population crossed the Mississippi River to enter Missouri.

Suggestions for Further Reading

Considering how old and significant Missouri is, surprisingly little of good quality has been written about her. Especially is this true concerning the century since 1875. Fortunately, in recent years the journals published quarterly by two historical societies in the state have often contained thoughtful essays which have touched even upon twentieth-century developments. A convenient way, therefore, to learn more about Missouri is to consult the *Missouri Historical Review,* organ of the State Historical Society of Missouri, located in Columbia, and the *Bulletin,* published by the Missouri Historical Society, with offices in St. Louis.

Some readers may find it more enjoyable to absorb a great deal about Missouri through a book prepared by the Missouri Writers Project of the Work Projects Administration. Although it is now a generation old, *Missouri, A Guide to the "Show Me" State* (New York: Duell, Sloan, and Pearce, 1941) is still filled with insights and much useful information about the state's character and achievement. This volume was largely the work of Charles van Ravenswaay, one of Missouri's sons who remained long enough to contribute handsomely to his state's culture before he, too, moved East.

The surveys of Missouri's history have suffered, as in so many other states, from the compulsion to write for the public schools or to mention as many locales and individuals as possible, since the market for state histories has traditionally lain in these directions. In spite of this handicap, Missouri has been the subject of some worthwhile general histories. For the best compilation of detail about Missouri in a single volume, readers should use Duane Meyer, *The Heritage of Missouri: A History* (St. Louis: State Publishing Co., 1973). Persons wishing for a vast amount of information will be grateful for David D. March's four-volume study, *The History of Missouri* (New York and West Palm Beach: Lewis Historical Publishing Co., 1967). An older, massive undertaking in five volumes is Floyd C. Shoemaker, *Missouri and Missourians: Land of Contrasts and People of Achievement* (Chicago: Lewis Publishing Co., 1943). Readers with serious interests will rely upon the results thus far in the series begun by the University of Missouri Press to mark the state's sesquicentennial. Of the five projected volumes three have appeared—William E. Foley, *A History of Missouri: 1673 To 1820* (Columbia: University of Missouri Press, 1971); Perry McCandless, *A History of Missouri: 1820 To 1860* (Columbia: University of Missouri Press, 1972); and William E. Parrish, *A History of Missouri: 1860 To 1875* (Columbia: University of Missouri Press, 1973).

After the path provided by these general studies, the road beyond becomes erratic and difficult. Good treatments of Missouri's several regions, for example, are scarce. The best volume on St. Louis, pleasing but superficial, is Ernest Kirschten, *Catfish and Crystal* (Garden City: Doubleday, 1960). Darrell Garwood, *Crossroads of America, the Story of Kansas City* (New York: W. W. Norton, 1948) is similarly helpful. A newly published interpretation of the state's fabled hill country is Russel L. Gerlach, *Immigrants in the Ozarks* (Columbia: University of Missouri Press, 1976), although anyone wishing to understand the region must still use Leonard Hall, *Stars Upstream: Life Along an Ozark River* (Columbia: University of Missouri Press, 1969). In a previous printing Hall's book was crucial in rousing interest in Missouri's waterways, leading eventually to the Ozark National Scenic Riverways legislation.

The earliest story of the Missouri country, concentrating on its natural charm, is retold in Marshall Sprague's handsome *So Vast A Land, Louisiana and the Purchase* (Boston: Little, Brown and Co., 1974). Those who seek the days when Missouri's location was especially significant will enjoy Robert L. Duffus, *The Santa Fe Trail* (New York and London: Longmans, Green, 1930) and Richard E. Oglesby, *Manuel Lisa and the Opening of the Missouri Fur Trade* (Norman: University of Oklahoma Press, 1963). The most spectacular physical event in the state's career is the subject of James Penick, Jr., *The New Madrid Earthquakes of 1811–1812* (Columbia: University of Missouri Press, 1976). One of the world's great rivers, and a source of pride to the state, is traced in Stanley Vestal, *The Missouri* (New York: Farrar and Rinehart, 1945).

There are some good books on Missouri's beginnings. The greatest of her Indian tribes is portrayed in John Joseph Mathews, *The Osages* (Norman: University of Oklahoma Press, 1961). Youthful Missouri's culture can be examined through John Francis McDermott, *Private Libraries in Creole St. Louis* (Baltimore: Johns Hopkins Press, 1938) and through two other volumes edited by McDermott, *The French in the Mississippi Valley* (Urbana: University of Illinois Press, 1965) and *Frenchmen and French Ways in the Mississippi Valley* (Urbana: University of Illinois Press, 1969). The full story of Missouri's admission to the Union is told by Glover Moore, *The Missouri Compromise, 1819–1821* (Lexington: University of Kentucky Press, 1953), while the furor that issue caused in the state is recreated in Floyd C. Shoemaker, *Missouri's Struggle for Statehood* (Jefferson City: Stephens Printing Co., 1916). Special features of Missouri's greatest days are studied in Timothy W. Hubbard and Lewis E. Davids, *Banking in Mid-America: A History of Missouri's Banks* (Washington: Public Affairs Press, 1969) and Louis C. Hunter, *Steamboats on the Western Rivers* (Cambridge: Harvard University Press, 1949).

Those who want to understand the struggling Missouri economy should read James Neal Primm, *Economic Policy in the Development of a Western State, Missouri, 1820–1860* (Cambridge: Harvard University Press, 1954) and James D. Norris, *Frontier Iron—The Maramec Iron Works* (Madison: State Historical Society of Wisconsin, 1964). Although much attention still must be given to the story of Missouri's blacks, the standard volume remains Harrison A. Trexler, *Slavery in Missouri, 1804–1865* (Baltimore: Johns Hopkins Press, 1914). Lewis E. Atherton, *The Frontier Merchant in Mid-America* (Columbia: University of Missouri Press, 1939 and 1971) attends not only to economic but also to social circumstances, and similar insights will be found in William Francis English, *The Pioneer Lawyer and Jurist in Missouri* (Columbia: University of Missouri Press, 1947); Frances Lea McCurdy, *Stump, Bar, and Pulpit: Speechmaking on the Missouri Frontier* (Columbia: University of Missouri Press, 1969); and William H. Lyon, *The Pioneer Editor in Missouri, 1808–1860* (Columbia: University of Missouri Press, 1965). Aspects of city development appear in Selwyn K. Troen, *The Public and the Schools: Shaping the St. Louis System, 1838–1920* (Columbia: University of Missouri Press, 1975) and in Charles N. Glaab, *Kansas City and the Railroads: Community Policy in the Growth of a Regional Metropolis* (Madison: State

Historical Society of Wisconsin, 1962). Although there is no major treatment of the Germans in Missouri, much about this topic appears in Henry A. Pochmann, *German Culture in America* (Madison: University of Wisconsin Press, 1957).

An excellent biography of Missouri's great senator is William N. Chambers, *Old Bullion Benton, Senator from the New West* (Boston: Little, Brown and Co., 1956). Life for the future Mark Twain and his family in Missouri is movingly portrayed by Dixon Wecter in *Sam Clemens of Hannibal* (Boston: Houghton Mifflin, 1952). The people of Missouri as seen in the work of the state's great artist are reproduced in E. Maurice Bloch, *The Drawings of George Caleb Bingham With a Catalogue Raisonné* (Columbia: University of Missouri Press, 1975). An admirable biography of the artist is John Francis McDermott, *George Caleb Bingham: River Portraitist* (Norman: University of Oklahoma Press, 1959).

A leader of the battle against Benton's ideas is the subject of William E. Parrish, *David Rice Atchison of Missouri* (Columbia: University of Missouri Press, 1961). Another kind of Missouri conservative appears in Marvin Cain, *Lincoln's Attorney General: Edward Bates of Missouri* (Columbia: University of Missouri Press, 1965). The Civil War era and its aftermath dominate two volumes by William E. Parrish, *Turbulent Partnership: Missouri and the Union, 1861–1865* (Columbia: University of Missouri Press, 1963) and *Missouri Under Radical Rule, 1865–1870* (Columbia: University of Missouri Press, 1965). What the Civil War meant to Missourians because of the vexations by Quantrill's and Anderson's irregulars is presented in Richard S. Brownlee, *Grey Ghosts of the Confederacy* (Baton Rouge: Louisiana State University Press, 1958).

There are several worthwhile biographies of Missourians who came to prominence during and after the Civil War. Robert E. Shalhope portrays one of the state's heroes in *Sterling Price: Portrait of a Southerner* (Columbia: University of Missouri Press, 1971), and Norma Peterson has considered Missouri's friend of reconciliation in *Freedom and Franchise: The Political Career of B. Gratz Brown* (Columbia: University of Missouri Press, 1965). Struggles for a better Missouri are recounted in George F. Lemmer, *Norman J. Colman and "Colman's Rural World": A Study in Agricultural Leadership* (Columbia: University of Missouri Press, 1953), and in Louis G. Geiger,

Joseph W. Folk of Missouri (Columbia: University of Missouri Press, 1953). The heroism of Missouri's great engineer is stressed in Florence Dorsey, *Road to the Sea: The Story of James B. Eads and the Mississippi River* (New York: Rinehart and Co., 1947). A vivid figure emerges in Max Putzel, *The Man in the Mirror: William Marion Reedy and His Magazine* (Cambridge: Harvard University Press, 1963).

For material on the recent travail in Missouri readers will have to depend largely on a few articles in the journals of the two historical societies. The definitive biography of Harry S. Truman remains to be written, although Jonathan Daniels, *The Man of Independence* (Philadelphia and New York: J. B. Lippincott, 1950) is still worth reading. However, the best picture of Truman and his Missouri will be found in Harry S. Truman, *Memoirs,* 2 vols. (Garden City: Doubleday, 1955–1956). A study of certain problems in Kansas City is Lyle W. Dorsett, *The Pendergast Machine* (New York: Oxford University Press, 1968). More general matters are covered in Franklin D. Mitchell, *Embattled Democracy: Missouri Democratic Politics, 1919–1932* (Columbia: University of Missouri Press, 1968). The work of Missouri's twentieth-century artist is beautifully reproduced in Matthew Baigell, *Thomas Hart Benton* (New York: Harry N. Abrams, Inc., 1973). Some of the writings of one of the state's leading scholars and educators have been edited with an introduction in Gilbert C. Fite, *Elmer Ellis: Teacher, Scholar, and Administrator* (Columbia: University of Missouri Press, 1961).

Index